THE DAMON RUNYON STORY

THE DAMON RUNYON STORY

BY ED WEINER

LONGMANS, GREEN AND CO.
NEW YORK · LONDON · TORONTO
1948

LONGMANS, GREEN AND CO., INC.
55 FIFTH AVENUE, NEW YORK 3

LONGMANS, GREEN AND CO. LTD.
6 & 7 CLIFFORD STREET, LONDON W1

LONGMANS, GREEN AND CO.
215 VICTORIA STREET, TORONTO 1

THE DAMON RUNYON STORY

COPYRIGHT · 1948

BY EDWARD H. WEINER

PUBLISHED SIMULTANEOUSLY IN THE DOMINION OF CANADA
BY LONGMANS, GREEN AND CO., TORONTO

FIRST EDITION

Printed in the United States of America

AUTHOR'S PREFACE

Damon Runyon left his biographers a slim legacy of facts concerning his early life. Although he used his own writing to create a literary fairground for exhibiting the personalities and daily living habits of his friends, the citizens of Broadway, and the people he came to know as a newspaper reporter, when his own life became a subject for examination he consistently practiced the strategic withdrawal. The author's research into Damon's childhood and adolescent years has provided a sequence of facts which form the foundation for the first section of this biography. But in order to give the book interest and continuity, the author has created the conversational scenes beginning in the first chapter, and continuing until Damon leaves Denver. The reader should understand, however, that these early scenes were carefully developed from the known biographical facts of Damon's life, and in no way distort his personality or character. The spirit of the biography has never been violated. As a friend of Damon Runyon's who studied his conversational style, and was deeply affected by his personality, the author believes the narrative scenes in the first eighty-four pages of the book to be accurate.

The author found it necessary in writing this book to enlist the help and cooperation of many other persons.

Grateful acknowledgment is made to Joseph Auslander, poet, novelist, and former Professor of Literature at Harvard and Columbia Universities, and his wife, Audrey Wurdemann, Pulitzer Prize-winning poet, for their invaluable assistance and interest in the preparation of the manuscript.

For his competent editing of the manuscript and his expert judgment, the author expresses deep appreciation to Francis Sugrue of the *New York Herald Tribune.* Thanks are also due Harold Flender for his initial work in the research.

For their generous help in supplying material concerning Damon Runyon's early life, the author is indebted to the following: Mr. L. T. Morgan, of Pueblo, Colorado; Mr. Stanley Lewis, of Beulah, Colorado; Mr. Willard B. Chappel, of Pueblo, Colorado; Mr. Edward H. Charette, of Stockton, California; Mr. Frank S. Hoag, of Pueblo, Colorado; Mrs. G. B. Harrop, of Manhattan, Kansas; and Mr. Robert E. Smith, of Sacramento, California. The author also wishes to thank Mr. Nyle H. Miller, managing editor of the *Kansas Historical Quarterly,* and the Kansas State Historical Society, of Topeka, Kansas, for furnishing the background material on the early history of the Runyon family.

Despite his terrific schedule of work hours, Walter Winchell was a source for a great deal of the material in these pages. The advice given by Irving Hoffman, drama critic of the *Hollywood Reporter,* is gratefully acknowledged.

Certain publishers, also, have been very kind in granting permission to quote liberally from Damon Runyon's writings, which have appeared from time to time under their imprints. Acknowledgment is made herewith to King Features for material that originally ran in Damon Runyon's column, "The Brighter Side," and for matter taken from other Runyon columns, here reproduced by permission of King Features Syndicate, Inc.; to Whittlesey House, for material quoted from *Short Takes*; to J. B. Lippincott Company, for quotations taken from *The Best of Runyon, Damon Runyon Favorites,* and *Trials and Other Tribulations*; and to Duell, Sloan and Pearce, Inc., for certain poems quoted from *Poems for Men*.

And finally, the author tips his hat in appreciation to the guys and dolls of Broadway, who not only shared their knowledge of Damon Runyon with the author, but play their parts in the cast of this book.

ED WEINER

To

MIM and JUNE

CONTENTS

PRELUDE TO "30"
by Walter Winchell

Tell 'em to lay off crying, Walter . . . A fellow ought
never to cry. When he does he can't see things clearly.
And if he sees things clearly he won't cry at all.

Look at it this way: A lucky Arabian Prince was born
with a magic carpet which took him everywhere. So,
what? It's no news that something extra was added for a
Prince . . . Who cares that there's a tassel on a gold spoon?

But take you and me, Walter. We were born into
Woolworth spoons—that is, when there was something to
eat . . . But we made a miraculous discovery. If we hadn't,
Alfred Damon Runyon would be just another name on a
rack near the time clock in the roundhouse of the Denver
and Rio Grande in Pueblo, Colo.; and you, well, who
knows? It was a miracle—that we discovered the miracle—
that a pen or typewriter will take you to every place a
Prince can go on a Magic Carpet—and a lot of places he
can't . . . It's a royal road you travel when you follow the
point of your nose by following the point of your pen . . .
I just figured that I was strictly a day coach guy in a parlor
car seat. So why should anyone be bawling when I'm not
squawking? . . . Just because they've called my stop doesn't
mean the journey is over . . . Why, the first thing I'm going
to do is thank the Great Conductor for a swell ride.

There are a few things I picked up on the trip which

may be useful . . . I always found that in a pinch one
ounce of understanding was worth a ton of sympathy . . .
Almost anybody will stand by you when you're right, but
it takes a real pal to stick by you when he thinks you're
wrong . . . I found, too, there isn't much difference
between the best of the worst and the worst of the best—
and about the worst fault of the best people is they think
there is. Their penalty for being Puritans is nobody tells
them the truth. Believe me, the one infallible formula for
getting the wrong slant is to look down your nose.

I tried to learn about people because in that way I could
find out about myself . . . I let the hometown papers take
care of the returning Local Boy who Made Good . . . I
just wrote about the local boys who went bad. There's
so much more material . . . The world calls them Broadway characters, but I knew the disappointment most of
them had to swallow did more to hurt them inside themselves than any pushing around anybody else could give
them on the outside . . . And I figured long after the world
has forgotten the laurel, an injured guy remembers who
loaned him a crutch. So they told me their stories and I
had the chance to tell them to the world. And to be kind
sometimes.

That's a great thrill! Under the rules of the game the
referee can only raise the hand of the winner. But the guy
with a typewriter can give a pat on the shoulder to the
kid they have to carry up the aisle . . . The title of a
champ is made in the ring, but believe me, the story of
the fight is in the loser's dressing room . . . I always made
it a point to talk to the losers to find out what they lacked
that the winners had. In most cases, it was luck.

Luck's a funny thing, Walter. It's true that some people work hard and never have it, but it's much truer that the blokes who won't work never have it at all . . . For every second a champ spends bowing before cheering thousands he spends days and weeks in the gym torturing himself alone . . . That's part of the price—and there's never a bargain sale . . . I guess that's true of everything. I used to wonder if the cops we followed on the short wave alarm realized that the words to describe the chase were as elusive as the shadows they were chasing.

Life itself is a risk, Walter—and you measure a man by the way he takes it . . . The bitter irony of it is the greatest risks are taken by people who think they are avoiding taking any risk at all . . . About the most dangerous thing a man can do, as any soldier knows, is to seek safety. Life is the game where you can't duck the odds by not taking a chance. But most people turn tail and then holler life has cheated them, just because it kicks them in contempt.

You can't shut the world out of your life by trying to shut your door on the world . . . It's true that to every man, woman and child, it's a different world. But the key to good writing, and other things, is that just where every-body thinks he's most different is where he's most alike . . . Take guys and dolls. When they're in love each thinks the one was born for the other. But the fact is any guy who wants to devote the time to it can usually capture a doll's heart—and vice versa. But the test of a thoroughbred is not how a heart is taken or even how it is used. It's how it's given back.

My world has been with People—and Words. Words are the tools of our trade and words are funny things. Add only one letter and you have swords—and often as not they cut as deep . . . Words can lift like a jet bomb and drop like a sashweight. An irresponsible reporter in front of a typewriter can do more damage than a drunken surgeon swinging a knife in the operating room.

I let historians live in the past and statesmen in the future . . . As a reporter it was my duty—and my good luck—to work in the present . . . Eternity and Utopia, I figured, were swell for the Sunday supplement—but it's the spot news that sells the paper . . . My world was bounded by the four corners of the Front Page and my horizons were its headlines . . . Because I believed in living in the present, I did the things I wanted to do when I wanted to do them. I figured what was my own business was not likely to be at anyone else's expense.

It's nice of you people to tell me now that I owe as few apologies—as I have regrets . . . As a matter of fact, I have none . . . Why, people were even thoughtful enough to print my obit, when I died, right on the Front Page, where I lived. That illustrates the most important thing Life ever taught me—that part of it was Death.

So, so long, Walter. Won't you give my deep thanks to the newspaper game for keeping its promise—that in it you never grow old. All reporters die at

"30"

[Reprinted through the courtesy of the *New York Daily Mirror*.]

PROLOGUE TO A NEWSPAPERMAN

The seven Renoyan brothers arrived in America from France a short time before the War of Independence began, and settled their families in Pennsylvania and New Jersey. One of their descendants was William Renoyan, a journeyman printer, who was born and raised in New Jersey. In 1852 William found his desire to seek the gold discovered in California stronger than his love for the security of the home he had built in the East. In New Jersey, New York, and Pennsylvania he found eighty

[1]

families who shared his restless hope for gold. But the ambition of these pilgrims of Midas was tempered by the stories of Indian massacres on the western plains. They reasoned that sudden death could be avoided in their journey for gold by finding an inland waterway to California.

In the early spring they boarded the steamer *Hartford* at Cincinnati, stowing all their worldly goods in the ship's hold, and keeping in their hearts an abundant faith in the cleverness of their design. The *Hartford* steamed down the Ohio River, up the Mississippi River, along the Missouri and Kansas rivers. It was August when they reached the mouth of the Blue River in Kansas and ran aground on a sand bar. The summer sun had dried up the waterway. A flat, dismal plain of buffalo grass stretched from the bow of their ship to the horizon: a barren symbol of failure.

The eastern gold-hunters decided to make this desolation of sun and grass their future. They unloaded their goods: the plows, the farm implements, the lumber. These were the tools of a new life. They built a settlement, and named it Manhattan, perhaps remembering the cool hills and protective mountains of the East, the soft, black soil. The buffalo grass of this Manhattan lay in solid mats six to eight inches deep. It took strength and courage to plow through these woven grass roots, to farm this land.

William Renoyan plowed a quarter section of buffalo grass and planted corn. When Manhattan began to print its own newspapers, he combined printing jobs with his farming, and changed the family name to Runyan. William had a son, whom he named Alfred Lee Runyan.

This lad was only thirteen when he began his newspaper career as an office boy for the *Manhattan Independent*. He cleaned the spittoons, swept the floor, and, from watching his father, soon learned to set type himself.

Kansas gained statehood in 1861. The population was divided over the issues of the Civil War, and punctuated their views on slavery and States' rights with violence and bloodshed. The Indians took advantage of this internecine struggle to raid the white man's villages, to destroy his property, to kill and maim his families. During these savage years, King Quantrill, an Indian leader who was proud of his reputation for inventing ingenious tortures for his victims, reigned over a vast domain of murder, kidnaping, and terror. His name was spoken in fearful whispers, and three states—Kansas, Missouri, and Kentucky—paid him gold as tribute. Alfred was sorry when King Quantrill was killed by a member of his own band in 1864. He had hoped to engage the Indian one day in hand-to-hand combat.

By the time he was seventeen years old, Alfred was not only able to set type, but was writing newspaper copy. He was now working for the *Manhattan Standard*. On October 10, 1868, a proclamation of the Governor of Kansas authorized the opening of recruiting offices for the organization of the 19th Kansas Regiment. Alfred enlisted on October 12, and was assigned to Company M of the 19th Volunteer Cavalry as a clerk. In November the regiment, led by General George Armstrong Custer, marched out on a six-month expedition against the Indians. Alfred had little regard for the famous Indian fighter, whom he disdainfully called "Custar." In the rather candid version of the expedition that he wrote for the *Standard,* Alfred reported caustically that more men of the cavalry were killed than Indians. He was particularly incensed because Custer had ordered the cavalry to dismount at Camp Supply, and to march twenty-five to thirty miles a day until they reached Fort Dodge. This was a case of utmost cruelty, Alfred said, because most of the men had blistered feet.

"Custar may gain a name for making long marches in short periods," Alfred wrote, "but he wears out men and animals in doing so. He has few friends among the privates of the 7th and 19th."

After Alfred was mustered out of the 19th Regiment he migrated to Junction City, Kansas, where he worked as an editorial writer for the *Junction City Tribune.* There he met Miss Libbie J. Damon, who had moved to Junction City with her family from Abilene, Kansas, in 1876. Alfred and Libbie were married on March 11, 1876, in Abilene, at the home of Libbie's sister, Mrs. A. O. Baldwin.

Alfred returned with his bride to Manhattan, where he published the *Manhattan Enterprise* in partnership with C. N. Patee. Five months later Mr. Patee resigned and Alfred became editor and manager of the paper. On October 8, 1880, the *Enterprise* published a notice: "Born, To A. L. Runyan and wife, October 3, a son." The Runyans named their son Alfred Damon and, to distinguish him from his father, they called him Al.

The *Enterprise* was sold in 1882, when Alfred and his family moved to Clay Center, Kansas, where Runyan and two other men bought the *Clay Center Times.* Three years later Alfred had shifted his allegiance from the *Times* to the *Clay Center Dispatch*. The Runyan partnerships never enjoyed a long existence. "Oh, how I envy the man who can enter into a partnership and make it an enduring success," Alfred moaned as one by one his business ventures dissolved. But the fluidity and instability of a newspaper fascinated him. A man could be publisher of a paper one day, typesetter the next, editor the third, and searching the "Help Wanted" notices the fourth. Alfred was familiar with all phases.

In 1885 the Runyans were on the move again. This time they settled in Wellington, Kansas, where Alfred entered into a newspaper partnership with four men. There he rented the largest mansion in town, bought new furniture, and was tailor-fitted for a frock coat. Since he and his partners owned two papers, Alfred reasoned that he was finally a newspaper tycoon. But the stability and respectability of a grand house could not quiet his restless spirit, nor tame his brusque tongue, and he soon was in trouble with his partners. First one resigned, and then A. J. Biddison, the man he had hired as business manager, brought suit against him on libel charges. Alfred was acquitted, but his own hot temper soon brought him again before the judge, when he tried to emphasize the judge's decision with his strong right fist.

In 1887, on the advice of the family doctor, Alfred moved his family, now increased by three daughters, to Pueblo, Colorado, where he took a job as a typesetter on the *Pueblo Chieftain*. His wife, Libbie, always a pale, slight woman, was believed to have "lung trouble," and the doctor thought the clear air of Colorado might improve her health. But the high mountains, reaching up beyond her hopes and experience, depressed her. She yearned for the warmth and comfort of the familiar and before long left Pueblo with the three little girls to visit her sister in Abilene. Before the year was over she had died of tuberculosis, and Alfred was alone with his son.

1

AL'S OLD MAN

Mrs. Morgan ran her wide, well-nourished hand along the gingham tablecloth, smoothing out the wrinkles. Then she set out two teacups, sugar bowl and cream pitcher, and half the chocolate layer cake she had baked that morning.

"I hope you don't mind having your tea in the kitchen, Mrs. Smith," she said to the small woman with a feathered hat who was peering through the rear window into the back yard where two small boys were playing.

"Oh, Mrs. Morgan now. I had no intention . . ." the

woman with the hat said, turning from the window and walking a few steps into the room. A clear spray of sun followed her steps, and grains of dust danced around the little woman's heels in the warm light. "I only dropped in to get acquainted, and not to put you to any trouble, now."

Mrs. Morgan listened politely to the expected protestations of her guest. "I'm always easier to get acquainted with over a cup of tea. I have some tea myself every day at this time, and I like to drink it here because the sun's in my kitchen in the afternoon."

"And the kitchen is your workshop, Mrs. Morgan. I always like to relax in my own workshop," Mrs. Smith said, sitting down to her cup of tea.

Mrs. Morgan picked two fine-cut glasses from a shelf and placed them on the table. "Would you like a sip of my elderberry wine with your tea?" she asked, pouring the dark liquid into the glasses.

"Well now," Mrs. Smith demurred, fingering her hat. "I don't usually . . . but it might be nice. Do you have wine yourself every afternoon?"

Mrs. Morgan laughed, her round, soft body quivering in echo to her amusement. "And why not? I make it with my own hands, so I believe I'm entitled to taste it with my own lips. I like to drink it here in the kitchen between washing my dinner dishes and preparing the evening supper. It makes me content with the world, and with Pueblo. Oh, Mrs. Smith, I think you'll like it here in Pueblo. We have the same good things you have in the East, and the air is so much better for you in Colorado."

"Well, if it's true about the Indians and badmen . . . and the saloons . . . I don't know."

"In all the time I've lived here, Mrs. Smith, I've never seen an Indian on the warpath, and I'm still waiting for my first glimpse of a real badman. When I do see one I intend to give him a glass of wine; that'll cool his temper."

The sound of playing boys came tumbling into the kitchen from the back yard.

"Are those your two boys in the yard?" Mrs. Smith asked.

"The taller one is my son, Tom; the other is Al Runyan," Mrs. Morgan replied, tasting her wine with pleasure.

"Seem like nice boys," Mrs. Smith commented quietly.

"Doesn't that poor Runyan boy look like a little ragamuffin?" Mrs. Morgan said.

Mrs. Smith's face brightened. "I was just going to say the scrawny little boy looked like a misplaced scarecrow. Why the tears in his pants and the filth of his shirt should be the shame of his mother."

Mrs. Morgan leaned across the table. "The lad has no mother. She was a frail little thing . . . didn't take to Colorado at all."

"What was it, t.b.?" Mrs. Smith almost whispered.

"Yes, a terrible thing," Mrs. Morgan whispered back. "And now poor Al is living with his father at the Mount Pleasant."

"Is that the boarding house?"

"It is. They only have one room and one bed. His father works at night on the *Chieftain* while Al is sleeping in the bed. And in the day the old man gets his rest while Al is scouring the town for mischief."

"His father is a saloon man, I suppose."

"Why, no, he's a newspaperman."

"He's always in the saloon drinking, that's what I mean," Mrs. Smith explained.

"He is. But he's a good man for all of it. He does his best, but how can a man raise a child by himself? You should see him strutting down the street all dressed up. He's a regular dude. He's a little man, you know, with red hair and a little beard. And he keeps the red tufts of his hair trimmed just so. Why I believe he shines his shoes every day."

"And leaves his son to go around like a ragpicker," Mrs. Smith said. "It's always that way when a man gets himself tied up with one of them loose women, with their hair all fluffed up and the eyes on them."

Mrs. Morgan laughed. "Oh, Mrs. Smith, you're making out Mr. Runyan to be a complete wastrel. He's like any other man I've ever known with the women—he takes his look."

The voice of a boy sounding a strange piercing chant echoed against the windowpane. "Wa-ooh, wa-ooh, wa-ooh, ya-ooh, ya-ooh, wa-oop, wa-oop, wa-oop," came the voice, filling the kitchen with its strident vibrations.

"Is that the Runyan boy?" Mrs. Smith asked.

"It's his voice. For pity's sake, the lad must be possessed."

Mrs. Smith scurried to the window. "Mrs. Morgan," she called in a soft hiss. "Come, take a look at this now."

Mrs. Morgan came to the window. Her eyes followed Mrs. Smith's pointing finger toward the far end of the garden where Al was prancing around the clothes pole in a frenzied dance. He crouched to the ground, pounded the earth with his fist, and then scampered along like an ailing chimpanzee. Now he leaped to his feet, and threw back his head. "Wa-ooh, wa-ooh, wa-ooh, ya-ooh, ya-ooh, ya-ooh, wa-oop, wa-oop, wa-oop," he screeched to the sky. Mrs. Morgan's eyes went to the clothes pole. A mound of leaves, barrel staves, and boxes was stacked neatly around the pole, and Tom Morgan, bound securely by a coil of rope, stood on top of the pile. A fire kindled among the leaves was now burning nicely among the barrel staves and wooden boxes.

Mrs. Morgan gazed at her son, who was peering into the fire as though hypnotized by the yellow flames licking their way toward his feet.

"Tom looks so lonely and lost," Mrs. Morgan murmured softly.

"Mrs. Morgan!" snapped the alarmed face under the hat.

Mrs. Morgan let out one brief scream of anguish. Then she grabbed a knife from the kitchen table and rushed into the yard. With two quick slashes she cut Tom's bonds and pulled him from the fire. The Indian dancer, with cautious wisdom, had moved to the other end of the garden to await developments. When Mrs. Morgan found Al, she pointed her knife toward him. A stream of invective followed the direction of the blade. But Al had little fear of words.

"I was just showing Tom how to play Indians just like they have in Kansas," Al replied coolly.

"Is that the way to play Indians, burning Tom at the stake? Al Runyan, where did you learn such roughneck games?"

"The cavalry was supposed to rescue him," he answered.

"You just went and spoiled the game. You didn't look like no cavalry coming to the rescue."

Mrs. Morgan communed quietly with her patience for a moment and then instructed the boys to get a bucket of water and put the fire out. When Tom and Al had reduced the fire to a mass of watered debris, the heat of Mrs. Morgan's fright and anger also subsided, and she ushered the two boys into her kitchen.

"Mrs. Smith, I want you to meet a young man who spends all his time with the Indians from Kansas when he should be giving more attention to washing away the dirt around his neck," Mrs. Morgan said, gently ushering Al into the kitchen. "He's been playing so hard at trying to turn my son into ashes he needs a glass of milk and a piece of cake."

Mrs. Smith stared at the slim, barefooted boy with distaste. Al returned her stare. "It's none of my business," she said, "but in my opinion this boy needs a stick across the knuckles more than he needs milk and cake."

Al moved to the table where Mrs. Morgan had set his milk and cake. "What didcha put in my milk, Mrs. Morgan?" he asked.

"Listen to him, will you? He thinks I've poisoned his milk," Mrs. Morgan said, laughing.

"He's got a wagging tongue on him, I'll say that," Mrs. Smith remarked.

"You've got a tongue always wagging yourself," Al replied.

Mrs. Smith was stunned into silence. She walked into the dining room, covering her retreat with expressions of gratitude for Mrs. Morgan's hospitality, the nice afternoon, the tea and cake and wine. She must get downtown to do her shopping, she explained. While Mrs. Morgan was escorting her guest to the front door, Al took the bottle of wine and refilled the two glasses, passing one to Tom.

"Drink it quick before your mother comes back," Al instructed. But Tom hesitated, for he was certain there was an element of sin and punishment involved in drinking his mother's wine.

"You gotta drink it 'cause you were rescued from the Indians," Al insisted. "When anyone's rescued from the Indians they drink stuff like this. . . . My father said so."

Al drained his glass first, and Tom quickly followed suit. The taste was new, both sweet and tart to their tongues; the two boys glanced at each other, and smiled, recognizing the pleasures of their secret wrongdoing.

Al liked Mrs. Morgan's kitchen; it was large, and comfortable and secure. It spoke of all the good things of home; the endurable, indestructible things of the family. He saw the shining blackness of the stove reflecting the kettle that rested contentedly on top, the large cat purring in the warmth of its sleep behind the stove, and the alcove on the far side of the room nesting a couch comfortable for the largest man. A bookcase stood behind the couch. Al regarded each book singly, and then in the unity of its row; the book covers were black and orange and red and green. The kitchen was centuries old in Al's memory, and now he was happy in this brief afternoon of time. He swung his legs under the table in a loose rhythm and let them bump against the rungs of his chair.

Mrs. Morgan returned to the kitchen. "Well, I see you routed Mrs. Smith without so much as a 'Good day to you ma'am'," she said, pinching Al's ear, and then filling both boys' glasses with milk.

"She's an old snooper, ma," Tom commented, "and she's got a chicken in her hat."

Al laughed so hard at Tom's remark that the cake he was chewing splattered from his mouth all over the table. Tom took a big bite of his cake and joined Al in the game of laughter.

"Enough of this nonsense, boys," Mrs. Morgan ordered with a sternness that denied any dissenting opinions. "You'll be laughing yourselves into convulsions, and besides I'll not have you treating my cake that way. . . . You have a right to your opinion, son, but it's too early to be telling anything about Mrs. Smith . . . we must be charitable. . . . But she made her points this afternoon. She said you needed a mother, Al, and I never heard truer words spoken outside the Bible. You need a mother like I need the stove in my kitchen."

"My mother's gone from here, ma'am," Al said respectfully. "She's gone to the Bible."

"I know she is, son, I know she is," Mrs. Morgan said with quiet sympathy. "Al, where does your old man feed you?"

"My old man, ma'am? You mean my father, Alfred?"

"I mean that little runt of a man with the red hair, and the red beard, and the voice that you can hear talking all over Pueblo. He's your old man, ain't he?"

Al made little effort to contain his glee. "I have an old man, I have an old man, I have an old man," he chanted in rhythm to his laughter. "My old man has a red beard, my old man has red hair, my old man has a red beard . . ."

"Al! Al! you mustn't be disrespectful to your father," Mrs. Morgan scolded.

"You said it first, Mrs. Morgan," Al reminded her.

"I guess I did. I shouldn't of, and neither should you. Well, where does your father feed you?"

Then it all came out. Al and his father ate wherever their fancy guided them. Al said he drank more coffee than milk, and sometimes, he said, they could hardly afford three meals a day.

Mrs. Morgan took that one in and felt impelled to learn more. Alfred Runyan, it appeared, was in the habit, at this time, of working for a month, drawing his pay, and then loafing until he and the boy were threatened with eating less than their customary three meals a day.

Mrs. Morgan made a sudden decision. Hers was a philosophy of motherhood that stretched beyond the walls of her own home and could easily include this wayward and unattached child. He was a good boy at heart, though she readily recognized his talent for getting into mischief and his inherent disrespect for adult regulations. But since these leanings were ordained by a divine instinct, Mrs. Morgan reasoned that they had already been accounted for and forgiven in heaven. She accepted children in their unrefined state of nature, and they understood her as a mother in reality. She sent the boys back to their play and told Al to return with Tom in the evening for dinner.

"And one more thing, Al, now listen carefully if you can hear through that pair of dirty ears."—Mrs. Morgan caught him as he was about to spring out the kitchen door.— "You come here for breakfast tomorrow, and you and Tom can go to school together. And tell that old man of yours that he can eat alone hereafter. You're going to eat at the Morgan house. Can you remember that?"

Alfred Runyan tipped the stout porcelain pitcher, and watched the water splash into the basin. "Every day I seem to pour out the same clear, cool water, filling the basin up to the crack," his thoughts said, running along the borders of his awakening consciousness. "It has no individuality, only unity. Look, it's settling now into a solid translucency, a paradox of fluidity and form. Oh, what a cold, unemotional, indifferent stuff—this water."

He cupped his hands and dipped cautiously into the basin, lifting the water to his face as he bent over the bowl. He bathed carefully, doing his best to keep his beard free of soapsuds. He was rinsing the soap from his cheeks when Al entered the room. Through the corner of his right eye, he peered at his son.

"Where the hell have you been, son, stealing chickens?" Alfred said, with feigned annoyance. "You let me sleep too long. Now it'll be eight o'clock before we get our dinner."

"I've already had my dinner, old man," Al said, moving over to the bed and sitting down. "The bed's nice and warm for me, ain't it, old man?"

"Old man who?" Alfred inquired, burying his face in a towel. "Old man me? Are you calling me your old man?"

"You're my old man, ain't ya?"

"I'm your father, Alfred Runyan, and it's a fine name, a strong, vigorous, unafraid, intelligent name. One to be proud of at all times. Although I'll have to admit it's a name that could fit an idiot just as well as a genius, and

I have my moments when I think it fits a jackass even better."

Alfred looked into the mirror to comb his hair, but the dark, reflected shadows of his own image distracted him. He walked over to the dressing table and turned up the wick of the kerosene lamp. The new, high flame, which drove back the shadows of the room, also sent up a current of black smoke. Alfred studied his features in the mirror again, patting his cheeks and chin tenderly.

"The light in this room is so poor you couldn't recognize a full-grown wart if it came up and bit you on the nose," Alfred said mournfully, abandoning the mirror. "So I'm an old man now. Where did you get the notion that you could call me 'old man'?"

"Mrs. Morgan. She said you were my old man and that you had a red beard and red hair."

"So it's old lady Morgan teaching you disrespect for your father," Alfred wailed, as he struggled to get into his trousers. "Old man . . . old man . . . old man, that's what she said I was. . . . Is that where you had your dinner?"

"Yeah, and I'm going to have breakfast there before I go to school tomorrow," Al continued excitedly, having just remembered the message he was to deliver to his father, "and Mrs. Morgan said that I was to board there, and to remember to tell you . . ."

"And to remember to tell me what . . ."

"And to remember to tell my old man that he was to eat alone 'cause I'm going to eat at the Morgan house."

The elder Runyan stared at his son, "So the old gal intends to take you over lock, stock, and barrel, does she?" he shouted, as he paced over the floor with quick, loping strides. "Did she also say I neglected you, beat you, locked you in your room, fed you bread and water, taught you how to steal, took you into saloons with me?"

"Mrs. Morgan said I needed a mother."

The fire of Alfred's temper suddenly cooled. For several minutes he studied the faded flower design in the bedroom rug. "Son, Mrs. Morgan is a good woman," Alfred said, as he resumed his pacing, now in slow, measured steps. "She's right, I am your old man. You call me your old man from now on, Al. . . . What is a parent anyway? A man or woman who has children? Oh, no, no. To be a parent you must have talent, a natural gift from God. Only a born parent can raise his family in the manner prescribed by civilized society. If we were animals—dogs or cats— it would all be simple; we would discharge our duty by instinct. I'm afraid that I've left myself open to criticism for the way I've conducted my tenure of parenthood. Mrs. Morgan would agree with me. Yes, Mrs. Morgan would agree, and she'd be right as the rain of spring. But Mrs. Morgan should know it's not all my fault. There are extenuating circumstances to be considered."

Although he knew his old man was not addressing him directly, Al listened intently, his eyes opened wide with wonder, his legs swinging back and forth in a pendulum motion as they always did when he was happy. He had seen his old man like this many times, striding around the room, talking and talking, alone in his soliloquy. It pleased Al to hear his father thus converse with the unseen world, for he knew it made him happy just to put his ideas into words.

"You take Grimes, he's a switchman on the Santa Fe,"

Alfred Runyan continued, quickening his step. "He has seven children and he has no more trouble bringing them up than if they were kittens. It's a pleasure and a wonder to go to his house and watch how gracefully he moves among his brood. What's his secret? By the Bible of the holy rock of ages, it's because he was born a parent. But take the person who's not a born parent and he'll have more trouble with one child than a dozen colds. And it's not how much you love your child that counts . . . Why, I know parents right here in this cursed town of Pueblo who love their children deeper than a well, but make a poor showing of bringing them up because they weren't born parents. And there are others who regard their children with affection as indifferent as a March morning but do a smart job of raising them. You know the answer . . . they're born parents."

Alfred turned to his son. "You tell Mrs. Morgan it'll be all right. She's one of those born parents. Just let me know what the board will cost me. . . . Now you'd better get to bed, son." Al's old man put on his hat and coat and left, closing the door gently behind him.

Al remained on the bed, listening closely to his father's steps as they went along the hall, moved quickly down the stairs, out the front door, and across the porch. Al's legs, which had ceased their swinging when his father left the room, hung limply from the bed. He shrugged his shoulders, hoping to cast off the loneliness that was settling over him, and walked across the room. He fingered the wash basin. It was decorated with bright red roses, and offered, rather heroically, the only symbol of cheer and hope in the room. The lamp chimney was now black with soot, and the darkness of the room encircled the lamp as though the feeble light were a helpless prey to be destroyed. Al blew out the light and turned toward the bed. To a boy just turning eight years old, the brown-painted, iron bedstead seemed cold, hostile, menacing.

It was nine o'clock when Al's old man entered the Arkansas Saloon. He walked hurriedly to the far end of the bar where a half dozen patrons were sipping beer. Pete, the bartender, glared at his new customer.

"What do you want, Gus, a hard-boiled egg?" Pete snarled. "We ain't got any hard-boiled eggs, only pickled."

Runyan tapped a coin on the bar. "It has always been my belief," he said, when he was sure he had the attention of the other patrons, "that time is an illusion, a mechanical device invented for the convenience of man. Look at him! Look at Pete, the hairy manlike animal who pours the drinks in this liquor emporium. He's the living proof of my theory on time. I was here twenty-four hours ago; I was here a week ago; I was here a year ago; and during all that time Pete's face has remained a fixed constant; a stone has more animation in time than Pete's face. His face has continued ugly as a boar's—depraved, perverted, degenerate, listless, and lustful. . . . As it was in the beginning, is now, and shall be unto eternity."

The row of faces along the bar laughed, but not boisterously, nor with full hearts; they remembered that Pete was in charge of the drinks on the house.

"You're right, Mack," Pete said. "Time is standing still. You're here five minutes by the clock already and haven't blasphemed against the Lord once yet."

"I'll get around to that, Pete."

"You're late getting here tonight," said Dick, one of the patrons. "What held you up?"

"Only the second coming of Christ could keep Runyan from getting his drink on time," Pete said.

"Christ will be able to come and go a half dozen times before I get a drink in here," Runyan shouted over the laughter.

Pete placed a beer before Runyan and then poured him a glass of whiskey. "Here's luck, Runyan," Pete said. "You saved me an hour of suffering by coming late tonight, so I'll give you the first one on the house."

"I forgot to mention that Pete has a heart of gold as well as an ugly countenance," Runyan said, lifting his whiskey glass to the level of his eyes in a toast to the bartender.

The men became silent and sipped their beer. Every saloon has its unexpected moments of quiet when the customers study their drinks intently as though the liquor held some secret they were trying to understand. It is almost a devotional period; perhaps the men pray, examine their consciences, or seek, in the inner recesses of their spirits, the answer to why they are standing in a saloon.

"Well, I see they buried Henry today," Pete remarked quietly. "He sure handed in his chips in hurry."

"It's a shame he went so suddenly," Patron No. 2 commented. "He was a good man."

"I was at his funeral this morning," Dick said.

"What do you mean he was a good man, and it's a shame? Bosh and nonsense," Runyan said, signaling to Pete for another drink. "He's no better in his grave than when he was alive, and he was certainly a sniveling, cheating scoundrel when he was walking on the earth befouling it with nefarious deeds."

The men shifted their positions, feeling the floor with their feet uneasily. Such words directed against the dead were a sacrilege, even if they were uttered in a saloon. They turned their eyes toward Runyan, hoping to see him wink, or make a sign that his remark was a joke. But his eyes were bright and clear; they all recognized the symptoms, and knew he was ready to defend and to argue his statement.

"But the man is dead, and buried," Dick pleaded, as though Runyan had not understood the condition of the man he had slandered.

"Exactly," Runyan snapped. "Why should we, the living, let a dead man make liars out of us? It grieves me as much as the next fellow to hear of someone dying, but I'll be damned if I see any sense in boosting a departed citizen who was a no-account when he was living. If you insist on being respectful toward the dead who were worthless when they infested our presence, then don't say a damn word about them. And you, Dick, what do you mean by going to his funeral? Only last week you were in here telling me what a dirty, low trick he had pulled on you. Do you think if he came back now he wouldn't be just as mean as he was?"

Alfred was warming to his subject when he noticed an ancient derelict wearing an oversized overcoat proceeding cautiously along the bar toward the men. His movements were as timid as a butterfly's, and he seemed prepared to run for the door at the first offensive remark. Pete gave the man a sign that he was not welcome.

"No, no, Pete, this honorable gentleman is my guest,"
Runyan protested. "Here is a man we should honor; an
honest, upright man who is not afraid to tell the world
where to get off. He does not care what men say about him
after he's dead, for they have said nothing good about him
while he was alive. He says fie on your mankind; he's
above us all. He has a free will, and he is the only independent man here tonight. He sleeps in hallways in the
winter, and on the hills in the summer; he eats what and
where he can, and he borrows his drink, but he will not
sacrifice his liberty for all the luxury in the world. His
reward is in heaven."

Runyan ordered drinks all around and when the whiskey
had been poured, he raised his glass. "A toast to the only
honest, independent man in Pueblo," he said. They all
drained their glasses. The derelict smiled sheepishly, and
politely removed himself from the group, going to a table
on the other side of the saloon.

Runyan began to talk now, on and on, with a rhythmic
sounding of words that shaped themselves into an ordered
series of ideas, stories, and philosophy, punctuated only by
the physical act of drinking. It was a typical Runyan pattern of conversation. During an evening he would castigate
the Cleveland administration in Washington, take a stand
against wife-beating, defend bankers, and pronounce men
to be worse gossips than women. He was an omnivorous
and impartial reader. He was well acquainted with the
works of Rousseau, Plutarch, Rabelais, and Homer. He was
fond of the novels of Balzac and Dickens, and could quote
from Shakespeare or Milton when he desired to underline
his point of view with more than his customary eloquence.

In his spare moments he read novels, magazines, and newspapers.

Runyan was just polishing off one discussion with a quote from the Bible when one of Pueblo's wealthy merchants walked into the saloon and stood at the other end of the bar. He ordered the best brand of whiskey in the house, and then called for drinks all around. The grateful patrons, except Runyan, nodded their appreciation to the merchant, and one by one they moved their drinks to his end of the bar. Runyan was left alone. The merchant told a joke, and a rolling thunder of laughter sounded through the saloon. Then he began his own pompous declamation of ideas and stories, while the patrons listened attentively. But Runyan never surrendered peacefully. He motioned the derelict to stand at his side and began reciting poetry, quoting from the classics in a loud, booming voice that completely drowned the oratory at the other end of the bar.

The tradesman looked toward the door as though he was expecting a policeman to enter momentarily to arrest Runyan. "How long has that guy been talking like that?" he asked the group of patrons.

"For centuries," one of them replied.

"Has he got a license for blowing steam in a public institution?" the merchant inquired, allowing a brief smile to show on the corners of his mouth. "Hey, you, whatever your name is down there," he called to Runyan. "Yes, you, you old windbag, why don't you put a cork in that mouth of yours?"

The patrons slapped each other on the back, and gleefully pounded the bar with their fists at this witticism. This was the opening Runyan had been seeking.

"So I'm an old windbag, am I?" Runyan began quietly. "Sure, I'll admit I'm an old windbag, but so is every politician, orator, and statesman in the country. But I don't claim any of the taxpayer's money for use of my wind. Do you know the meaning of 'windbag'? No, because you are the worst sort of windbag; your wind has no juice in it. I've been quoting from Shakespeare, Paine, Voltaire, and Rousseau, while you've been quoting from the lean, undernourished thoughts in your feeble mind. Why, my poor befuddled man, you think you have a reputation as a thinker. You never had a thought that was worth two cents—in Mexican money. These people do not lend their ears to hear the pearls of wisdom that you think are spouting from your mouth. Ask them. They're listening to the gold that jingles in your pocket. I will give you a piece of wisdom to take home to your feather bed tonight. The only difference between a windbag and a man of wisdom is the money in his pocket."

When Runyan reached the *Chieftain* building that night he found his son crouching in the doorway. "Where've you been, old man?" Al inquired, stretching himself out to his full size. "I've been waiting here for you."

"What the hell are you doing here, Al?" Runyan asked impatiently. "I told you to go to sleep."

"I was sad there, old man," Al said in a small, almost sobbing voice. "It was dark, and I didn't want to stay there any more. I guess maybe I was a'scared."

Runyan placed his arm over Al's shoulder and led him up the stairs into the *Chieftain*'s pressroom. The elder Runyan formed a makeshift bed out of newspapers and coats under the table where he worked. "Crawl in there, son," he said gently, "you won't be all alone now. The whole damned world will be here with you, going to press."

Al smiled and crawled into his bed. He fell asleep to the clattering lullaby of the presses and the general hubbub of a newspaper office preparing its morning edition.

2

SMOKER AT 9; REPORTER AT 15

The day Al began boarding at the Morgan house he was handed a towel, and a wash cloth trimmed with a blue border. Mrs. Morgan attached a safety pin to the corner of the towel. "This pin makes the towel yours," she said, "and you'll always find it, and the wash cloth, too, on the rack in the kitchen, ready to be used before and after every meal."

Al was so proud of his wash cloth that he strove to keep it neat and fresh by economizing on its daily use.

For a time Mrs. Morgan accepted with patient interest the fact that Al's dirty hands and face remained unchanged. Then, realizing that his tolerance of dirt was due to ignorance rather than stubbornness, Mrs. Morgan schooled him in the blessings of hot water and made him promise to abide by the family rules for daily bathing. On Mondays Al's clothes were piled with the Morgan wash marked for extra scrubbing and a half-hour's steaming in the copper boiler. On Tuesdays his torn shirts and ragged trousers were laid in a neat stack near Mrs. Morgan's sewing box. She said that it was her opinion that clean and orderly clothes helped to build a boy's character.

Mrs. Morgan was happiest when Al used her back yard as a base of operations. She could then oversee his activities and protect her own flesh and blood when Al's idea of fun jeopardized the life and limbs of his playmate. One afternoon a period of silence in the back yard attracted her attention. When she looked out the kitchen window, she saw Al standing at the other end of the yard holding a bow in his hand, and aiming an arrow toward the house.

Mrs. Morgan opened the window and scanned the yard in search of Al's target. She found it under the window. There was Tom, standing stiff and straight, balancing an apple on his head.

"Al Runyan, what on earth are you doing?" Mrs. Morgan cried, shaking her finger vigorously in his direction. "Shooting at Tom and putting his eye out?"

"I ain't put Tom's eye out," Al objected. "We're just playing William Tell shooting the apple off the kid's head like it says in our reading book."

"Well, I'll *tell* you something! You just put that bow and arrow away and stop that game," Mrs. Morgan said sternly.

Tom looked up at his mother with a pained and hopeless expression. "Ah, ma, he's only got one more arrow to shoot and then it's my turn," he said. "Yuh never let me have any fun." But Al readily agreed that Mrs. Morgan had a point in her argument and said he was willing to quit the game. It was a part of Al's philosophy never to make a target of himself voluntarily.

Al and Tom, along with Ben Lear * and Stanley Lewis, were the leaders of a gang of boys who made their headquarters downtown in the doorway of the *Chieftain* building. The gang met here to design the strategy for each day's adventure. The peaceful citizens of Pueblo viewed the activities of the gang with skepticism, if not with alarm, for it was commonly known that the fun these boys generated was seldom innocent. One day they would invade Pueblo's wealthy residential section to war against the children of the rich; the next day they would send a raiding party into a neighborhood orchard, or schedule a sortie against a drugstore, a novelty shop, a fruit or candy store. All goods not protected by a locked door, a watch dog, or a wary citizen were considered fair plunder for the gang's marauding.

Although Al wasn't the leader of the gang because he wasn't the biggest tough, he was their idea man. He designed the plots and acted as chief counselor in all undertakings. He possessed the imagination for creating mischief and excitement, while the other boys contributed

* Later General Ben Lear of World War II fame.

their strength and will in carrying out his ideas. When the details of the day's enterprise had been decided upon, Al retreated to the sidelines to observe the activities. Since he was the gang's field general and chief tactician, he believed he was too valuable to be injured in a fight, or captured on a dangerous mission by an alert adult.

One day the gang sat on the bench in front of the *Chieftain* debating the quality and degree of their courage, each boy reciting the details of one of his acts which he considered a triumph of valor. When it came to Al's turn to relate his most daring feat, he startled the group by stating that he was the bravest of them all. Not only did this rouse the others to high indignation, but they refused to accept Al's statement at its face value.

"What do you mean, you're so brave?" one boy demanded. "Did you ever fight Big Slim like the rest of us?"

"Yeah, and you all got licked, too," Al sneered. "What's brave about that? That's just dumb."

"Would you ever jump off the bridge into the Arkansas River?"

"I would like hell, unless my pants were on fire."

"Would you catch a runaway horse, and try to bring him down?"

"Not unless he caught me first," Al replied, and countered with his own question. "Did any of you guys ever cut your initials in a church steeple?"

The gang realized that Al had scored a point for his case. It was well known around town that he had climbed to the steeple of the adobe church at Seventh and Main Streets to impress a young girl with his courage and had taken advantage of this opportunity to cut a large set of initials in the church belfry.

But the gang was not satisfied that this one feat made Al their better in courage. They flooded him with questions, aimed at disproving his claim. "Would you go into a grave-yard at midnight?" . . . "Would you fight a duel with real bullets in the gun?" . . . "Would you climb up on the Widow's roof and peek into her window when she was dressing?"

When the torrent of questions began to subside, Al raised his hand for silence. "I'll prove to you right now that I'm the bravest. I'll do something all of you are scared to do. I'll smoke a cigarette right here on the street."

The gang was impressed, for none of them dared to smoke a cigarette, except in a safe hiding place, or when they were walking deep in the hills where they were sure no one would see them. But Al always carried a package of cigarettes in his pocket, although until now, as a conces-sion to his nine years, he had always been discreet about where he did his smoking.

"You're just a great big bluff," one of the gang said. "I'm getting wise to you."

"You're loony, Al," another cautioned. "Every jackass and his brother will see you if you smoke here."

"Are you going to do your smoking trick?" Tom Morgan asked.

Al made no answer. Instead, he walked to the center of the street, took out his package of Duke cigarettes and placed one of them in his mouth. The gang crowded around him.

"Scatter out, scatter out," Al ordered, lighting the cigarette. "Make room for the customers who'll want a good look."

Al didn't have to wait very long. He had taken only a few puffs on his cigarette when two patrons from the Arkansas Saloon stopped to watch him.

"Hey, misters," Tom shouted to the men, "watch how he smokes, watch him!"

Al took a drag on his cigarette. He allowed the smoke to drift out of his mouth and up through his nostrils.

"See it, see it going up his nose?" Tom yelled excitedly. "Now watch, now watch."

Al then inhaled and blew it out his mouth.

"See? See?"

"Well, I'll be damned," one of the men said. "Did you see that? He did a complete circle with that smoke. In his mouth, up his nose, and out of his mouth again. How do you do it, son, with mirrors?"

"Say, isn't that old man Runyan's kid?" the other man suggested.

"Damn if it ain't. Hey, son, you're a credit to your old man. He'll sure be proud when he hears about this."

Al assumed a pose of complete indifference. He tilted his head slightly when he blew out the smoke, and rested the palm of his left hand lightly on his left hip.

Al was completely surrounded by adults and children now. He lighted a fresh cigarette, and performed his trick again. The crowd applauded. A woman edged her way into the inner core of the circle, and an uneasy murmur ran through the crowd. It was Mrs. Smith.

"I knew it, I knew it," she said in a shrill voice. "It's that Runyan boy smoking a cigarette in public . . . what a shame, and you men laughing and clapping, and not one of you turning a hand to stop this disgrace! Here, boy, give me that cigarette."

"Go away, you old sourface," Al said, now alive with anger because his show had been broken up. "Go home, you old snooper, and take your nose out of my affairs."

A burst of guffaws and snickers greeted that retort.

Mrs. Smith parried the crowd's insolent stares with a look of hot indignation.

"If you had a man for a father," she said, her voice full of fury, "he'd thrash you within an inch of your life."

"Why would this boy's father thrash him within an inch of his life?" a calm voice asked. It was Alfred Runyan. He had moved through the crowd, and was now standing beside his son.

"You see that cigarette in his hand? Did you hear what he called me? Do you know your duty?"

"Why you pinched-faced, frustrated old sow," Runyan said, "you are causing all this trouble because you can't smoke one of these cigarettes yourself." Runyan grabbed Al by the arm and ushered him through the crowd, keeping a firm grip on his son as he hurried him toward the Mount Pleasant.

One early evening in spring old man Runyan was striding down Main Street toward the Arkansas Saloon when the sight of a comely woman on the other side of the street made him slow down considerably. One of the most satisfying of the few freedoms in life was the right to look at a fair lady. This woman was dressed in good taste and carried herself with a dignified pleasantness. Runyan recognized her. Al had pointed her out one day as his teacher at the Hinsdale School. Runyan crossed the street and introduced himself to the lady, remarking that he hoped to combine the business of being a parent with the pleasure of talking to a pretty young lady. The teacher smiled and said she was always happy to meet the parents of her pupils.

"But I must tell you the truth, Mr. Runyan," she remarked. "I don't see too much of your son, for half the time he doesn't come to school at all."

"I can understand a boy's instincts rebelling against the discipline of school," Runyan said, "but now that I have met his teacher I find his absence from school extraordinary, if not unnatural."

The pretty teacher blushed. "I believe Al thinks he's a better teacher than I am; at least he has done a remarkable job of teaching the other boys to smoke and to use profane language. . . . Mr. Runyan, I, too, know something of the natural instincts of boys. I realize that all boys express themselves in a vigorous language when they are at play. . . . But Mr. Runyan, the words Al uses! . . ."

Runyan covered his face with his hand to hide a smile and was silent for a moment. His son was a master in the use of profane language, believing that the expressive, short words, if not dulled by overuse, were the most effective weapons available in his verbal combats with the town merchants and other citizens who proved intolerant of his activities. But Runyan believed that he was duty bound to defend Al.

"I'll speak to Al about his language," he said, "but I doubt if it will do much good. There are certain ideas that spring into the mind from time to time that can only be expressed with these ... ah ... er ... these words. During my lifetime I have made attempts to substitute milder, politer words for the offensive ones, but this only led to frustration, and an unnatural deceit on my part. . . . Hasn't Al done anything at school that would be a credit to him? And perhaps to his father?"

"Well, Al is an excellent speller," she said with enthusiasm. "He and Tom Morgan are the best spellers in the class; neither boy has made a mark under 100 all year."

"Why, that's as fine as grass. He'll be a writing man."

"That son of yours is already a writing man—but a destructive one," the teacher said. "Most of the woodwork in Hinsdale School is decorated with his initials."

Runyan laughed, and even the pretty teacher smiled. "Yes, Al has developed quite a habit of carving his initials in Pueblo wood. Why, I guess you can find 'A.D.R.' all over town. He likes to carve them in inaccessible spots as a sort of challenge to all Pueblo."

"I think Al lives too much in his imagination . . ." the teacher suggested.

"Too much in his imagination, poppycock!" Runyan replied. "Where else should a boy live but in his imagination? He'll discover reality all too soon when he has to earn a dollar. . . . Some of those sacred tenets in your school copybooks are nothing but booby traps. . . . Take that one, 'Habit is a cable—we weave a thread of it each day and at last cannot break it.' "

"And how true that is, Mr. Runyan," the teacher said.

"Truth! A fool's truth," Runyan said. "It's a defeatist theory aimed at destroying a youngster's confidence.

Every blessed mite of a child among us acquires his bundle of bad habits when he's growing up. What happens if he's taught he can never be free of his bad habits? Why, he doesn't try! He'll carry them around with him for the rest of his life, a burden to himself and a nuisance to his family. During my life I reckon I've picked up a bundle of bad habits. But I've been able to pawn most of them off, because I've had faith in my ability to do so."

Runyan tipped his hat and bid the teacher good evening. She said she had been pleased to meet Mr. Runyan, but could hardly subscribe to his views on teaching, nor would she expect any changes in Al's conduct as a result of their conversation.

On early summer evenings the gang would sometimes leave off their shenanigans to climb the slope of a near-by hill that shouldered the town like a friendly neighbor. The boys would lie on their backs to watch the clouds run across the open span of darkening sky. Each would name a cloud as his own and bet that it would be the first to disappear over the hills that stood like black, projecting fingers on the other side of town. As one set of clouds disappeared, another formed overhead, and a new game would begin.

When they tired, Al would point to the floating clouds. "See them, they're going to Kansas." The other boys would place a few stalks of grass in their mouths, savor them with their tongues, and relax against the earth. Al was going to tell a story and they always listened to Al.

He reminded the gang that the biggest and fiercest Indians came from Kansas, and that both he and his old man had been born in Manhattan, Kansas. He told them that his old man had fought against the Indians: the Cheyennes, the Arapahoes, the Kiowas, the Comanches, and the Apaches. If the evening wind were fresh and cooling, and Al were on good terms with his father, he would expand his tale to describe how King Quantrill, the Indian born of the devil, had come to his untimely end. In a soft, convincing voice, Al would recount that his old man was only nine years old when he met King Quantrill face to face in mortal combat. Armed with only a knife, Al said, his old man killed the savage with two blows and then ran away with King Quantrill's scalp.

Now the sky was dark, black on top and green near the edges, forming a backdrop for the early stars. In Pueblo the yellow light of oil lamps dotted the night, spreading a pattern of warmth and comfort. But on the hill near the stars the boys found in their imagination a world of song and adventure that reached into infinity; it was a world they could project into the future or back into the memory of the past.

The night came but the boys continued to talk. Later they could descend into the harbor of their homes, resume their games and old haunts. Al could return to his home: one room and an iron bed. He urged the gang to linger, convincing them that the night and the stars would make them tellers of stories, prophets and dreamers of the ages.

Al had inherited his father's talent for telling tales, and he became known as the boy storyteller of Pueblo. When he was thirteen years old he began forming his tales into written compositions and showing them to his father. Runyan was temporary editor of *The Pueblo Colorado Adviser,* a commercial weekly, and he considered two of his

son's pieces so well written that he inserted them in the
paper under Al's own name. One of the pieces was a report
of a lynching. The other was a short yarn about a kindly
physician named Doc Brackett, who cared for more people
than any other doctor in town, but made less money because he ministered to so many poor people. He answered
every call and would drive twenty miles on the coldest
night of the year to attend a sick woman or a child, or to
treat some fellow who had been injured in the factory or at
work in the fields. According to the story, Doc Brackett's
office was over a clothing store, and a sign at the bottom
of the stairs pointed to the waiting room. When Doc
Brackett died, the townspeople talked of raising enough
money to place a nice tombstone on his grave, but nothing
was ever done about it. One day word that Doc Brackett
now had a fine memorial over his grave spread around
town. A Mexican family, whose child had been saved by
Doc Brackett had removed the office sign and placed it
on the head of his grave. The sign, with the finger of the
hand pointed toward the sky, read, "Doc Brackett, Office
Upstairs."*

---

* Fifty years later, when Al's name had been changed to Damon
Runyon, the Doc Brackett story became the center of a minor literary
controversy. The story appeared in a Damon Runyon collection of short
yarns entitled *In Our Town*. Immediately scores of persons from all parts
of the country, who had either heard some version of the story at a
community dinner, or had read it in a magazine or local newspaper,
challenged Runyon's right to use the story, and suggested that he might
be guilty of plagiarism. It seems that Doc Brackett, sometimes under a
different name, had become part of the stock in trade of after-dinner
speakers. Damon, who admitted that he did not create the facts in the
story, said his father had told him the tale. But he pointed out that anyone who accused him of plagiarism, or wished to claim literary priority to
the piece, would have to produce a printed version of the story that was
over fifty years old.

Two years after his first stories were published, Al began his newspaper career as a reporter for the *Evening Press,* which had its offices in the south side of Pueblo. His boss was Colonel W. B. McKinney, an editor who believed that the most important words in the English language were over-ripe adjectives ready to sour, and that the proper way to speak this language was in a booming bellow. Colonel McKinney had an instinctive dislike for many of the town's leading citizens, and one of his greatest pleasures was nurturing these enmities into pet hates. Reporters on the *Evening Press* found it expedient to accept their editor's hates as their own, and Al, who was learning to play the chameleon whenever it suited his purpose, had little trouble in reflecting Colonel McKinney's personality.

The Colonel had a particularly strong dislike for John H. Mitchell, the county judge. In writing a routine, three-paragraph story on a case that had been tried before Judge Mitchell, Al one day referred to him as "Judge Johnny-hmitchell." When Colonel McKinney received the story at his desk, he sprang from his chair and let out an ejaculation that stopped the presses.

"Here, all you liver-shrunk gophers," he shouted, waving the story in his hand, "I got the best story since the Resurrection. And it took that young punk Runyan to do it. . . . Judge Johnnyhmitchell . . . ha, ha, ha, ha. . . . Runyan, you wet-washed little beggar, you get a two-dollar raise for this."

The Colonel spelled out Al's version of Judge Mitchell's name, and instructed all his reporters to copy it down. Every time they mentioned Judge Mitchell in a story, they were to use this style for spelling his name.

"And, Runyan, you cadaverous gargoyle, I want you to go down to the courthouse every day, and dig up a story in which you can use Mitchell's name. I want his name that way in the paper every day we go to press, rain or shine. If you can't find anything else, get a story on what he eats for breakfast."

One day the Colonel was standing before a bench setting one of his editorials in type by hand when Al rushed into the office, and headed for his desk.

"What's the matter, Runyan?" Colonel McKinney asked. "Did a real news story bust in your rat-picked face?"

"Colonel, I think I've got a good story," Al replied, meekly.

"A good story, eh?" the Colonel barked. "Did Judge Mitchell break his leg? I'll tear out the whole front page for that story, Runyan."

"It's a front-page story in my opinion," Al said. "It's a human-interest story."

The Colonel winced. "Probably the only human being on the face of the earth interested in the story is yourself," he said.

"It's about two kids, a boy and a girl, who fell through the ice into the river," Al related, certain that the Colonel's interest would be aroused when he heard the facts. "The kids had a dog with them, and the dog began running up and down the ice, barking like hell was on fire until he attracted the attention of some people passing by. And then the dog ran out to the hole in the ice and grabbed the kids' coats in his teeth and held them up in the water until help came. . . . Let me write it up for you."

"Write it up?" Colonel McKinney shouted with contempt. "Come over here, you chicken-brained runt. A good reporter is able to carry his whole story in his head."

Al walked over to the Colonel's bench. "Do you see that?" the Colonel said, waving his hand toward a case of type. "I just set up my editorial right out of my head. I didn't have to write it up first. Go ahead. Spiel out your piece of fiction, I'll set it up in type."

Al had already formed the lead for his story in his mind. "The darkened shadows of winter evening were falling over the Arkansas River yesterday when . . ." he began. The Colonel waved his hand for Al to stop.

"If you perused our paper with any sort of assiduity, Mr. Runyan," the Colonel remarked sourly, "you would know that the Poetry Society meets at 7:30 tonight in the high-school auditorium. It may be, Mr. Runyan, that you missed your calling in life when you decided to be a reporter. We in the newspaper business, Mr. Runyan, are interested in facts."

"But I thought a little life and color . . ." Al pleaded, in a feeble voice.

"Perhaps you had better visit one of the madams," the Colonel said, "if you want to get some of that life and color out of your system. Go on with your story."

Al was halfway through the story when he was stopped again. "Mr. Runyan, about this dog," the Colonel said. "Was it a big dog, or a little dog?"

"Well, er, why, ah, it was a medium-sized dog, I guess," Al mumbled.

" 'A medium-sized dog, I guess'," the Colonel repeated. "I take it that this forthright statement means that the dog was big enough to attract the whole countryside barking like all the hounds of hell, but not so big that he'd fall through the thin ice. And how many sets of teeth did this dog have? Two? It would be a remarkable dog that could hold up two children with one set of teeth. And, Mr. Runyan, did you talk to the people who rescued the children?"

"Why, no," Al answered sheepishly.

"Did you question the police?"

"No, I guess not."

"Did you interview the children?"

"Well, not exactly."

"Why, you wooden-headed, pimple-brained boob!" the Colonel shouted, waving his hands around like a windmill. "That's the trouble with all you fledgling reporters. You're still wet behind the ears. What do you think this is? A glue factory? You think all newspapers should be made up of ten per cent fact and ninety per cent reporters' deathless prose. . . . Go on with the story, the readers will probably eat your stuff up."

At this time Al was receiving rich experience in the basic and necessary ingredient of all newspapers—violence: the daily stories of murder, rape, robbery, and lynching. Al never forgot the time Dave Allen, one of the brothers who operated the Home Café, a saloon on Main Street, was stabbed to death by a Negro in the barroom of the Grand Hotel. The Negro escaped, but was later captured in Denver, and a lynching mob was organized to meet the train that was to bring him back to Pueblo. In the excitement and confusion of the darkness they slipped the rope around the neck of Miles Saunders, the district attorney, and almost lynched him by mistake.

In the accepted tradition for reporters at this time, Al worked at least once for every paper in town. No self-respecting newspaperman cared to remain on one paper for any extended period of time. Drinking was the cause of a great deal of the fluidity in the newspaper business. Reporters were frequently fired for drunkenness, and just as often a reporter would quit in the throes of a hangover, when he could no longer absorb the verbal abuse of his editor.

By this time Al had added drinking to his list of vices. He was considered a steady customer at the Home Café, where all the bartenders knew what he wanted, and poured his drink for him without asking any questions as soon as he stepped to the bar. Al was quite proud of the fact that he was accepted at the saloon and took other steps, cautious and tentative at first, to establish his manhood. Soon he was joining in the conversations about women with the authority of a man who had experienced all the pleasures man is able to enjoy. For a time Al believed that he held the world in the palm of his hand, but then he became restless, and his mind was disturbed by a persistent feeling that the world might be bigger than the Home Café, the town newspapers, the women he knew—bigger, even, than Pueblo.

3

THE MAINE, A BLOW PIPE, A POEM

At 9:40 P.M., on February 15, 1898, the United States battleship *Maine,* which had been anchored in Havana Harbor to protect American interests from the turmoil of the native Cuban insurrection against Spanish rule, was blown up and sunk, drowning or killing 260 of the 350 enlisted men and officers aboard. Americans were shocked at the news, and their indignation mounted to an angry and persistent call for revenge against Spain. Throughout the country American men, with red faces, flashing eyes,

[44]

and determined chins, all eager to shoulder a rifle, were attempting to volunteer their services to fight against Spain.

Al was now working for the *Pueblo Evening Post*, but he hadn't been able to escape from the tutelage of Colonel McKinney, who had also changed his newspaper allegiance, and was now editor for the *Post*.

"Well, Runyan, it looks like I'll have to reprint all those dastardly things I wrote about Judge Mitchell," Colonel McKinney said one day after the *Maine* sinking. "I'll just substitute the word 'Spain' for Judge Mitchell, and every home-loving citizen will think I'm the greatest American patriot of them all."

"You can get nastier than that, Colonel," Al remarked. "This is the chance of your life. You can say anything you please about a Spaniard, and no one will threaten to sue you or shoot you."

"I find it hard to get up a sweat for vilifying someone I don't know," the Colonel replied sadly. "I like to attack individuals, not a whole bellyful of people. I suppose I'll have to be nice to you drooling punks if you're going off to war. Most of you'll probably get your rear ends shot off." He picked up a late wire. "I like this story from New York. It says a group of businessmen calling themselves 'five hundred sharpshooters made up of Westchester businessmen' have attempted to sign up."

"That's what we ought to do around here," Al declared firmly.

"Yes, it's certainly an inspiration to a man's courage when he knows there is no authority to accept the volunteers," the Colonel remarked, with a soft taste of bitterness. "Runyan, why don't you get yourself a job as a war correspondent; get to see the world, and maybe you'll learn to spit over your chin."

"I'm going to fight in this war," Al said in a voice hoarse with dignity. "I'm going to carry a gun like the rest of them."

"How brave, how very brave of you," the Colonel said, innocently. "You're too young to die, but certainly ugly enough."

Congress declared war on April 25. The proclamation read that a state of war had existed between the United States and Spain since April 21.

The opening of the recruiting offices in Pueblo, accompanied by the playing of vigorous martial music, and the airing of patriotic speeches, reminded Al of Independence Day; the prevailing spirit of good-natured frivolity was like Christmas Eve. When Al walked into the Home Café, the saloon was crowded, filled with noise, smoke, and laughter. Al had to call out for his drink; the bartenders were so busy they had no time to recognize customers. Al's friends were centered around the middle of the bar.

"Come down here, Runyan," Joe, one of his friends, called. "Tomorrow we enlist; we put away the things of childhood; tomorrow we are armed with a spear. Are you going to join us tomorrow?"

"I'll be there tomorrow when the bugle blows," Al said, moving down the bar. "I'll be marching along with you, but I don't have to brag about it today to convince myself I'm brave; I'll just drink."

"Hey, listen to the tough guy, will ya," Joe remarked,

giving Al a gentle poke in the ribs. "Listen, Runyan, old man, let me tell you something confidentially: I heard the Spaniards have guns, and they shoot real bullets in them."

"What does Al care about bullets?" Tom said. "Remember how he used to smoke on Main Street?"

"Yeah, but he still hasn't had a fight with Big Slim," Bill said.

"And you guys still haven't licked him," Al retorted.

The friends laughed, slapped each other on the back, and Al ordered another round of drinks. Groups of men at each end of the bar had formed in circles, strangers and friends milling together in a common fraternity. One group was singing; another was watching a man give a pantomime demonstration of how to load a rifle. He made many mistakes, and his circle laughed its appreciation at this burlesque. Then the man crouched to his knees and shuffled his way along the bar, indicating through his gestures that he was about to attack a fortified position. His target was the jar of pickled eggs at the end of the bar.

"Hand them over," he said to a bartender, pointing his imaginary gun at the jar.

The bartender, receiving a nod from the owner of the saloon, pushed the jar toward the man, who then picked out the eggs one by one and threw them high in the air toward the circle of friends at the other end of the bar. Many were caught, but some of them splattered on the coats of the customers, the yellow and white pieces falling to the floor. Al leaped high in the air, grabbed one on the fly, wolfed it in two bites.

"That Runyan has the appetite of a horse," Bill said, as he watched Al wash the egg down with his drink.

"Al's just a growing boy," Tom remarked.

"Yeah, just a growing boy," Joe said, suspiciously. "How old are you, Runyan?"

"I'm eighteen," he answered, worried.

"You are like hell," Joe said with glee. "I was in school with you. Your birthday was in October just like mine. And it used to make you sore because I was a year older than you. And I'm eighteen."

"Hey, Runyan's not old enough to join the army," someone shouted. The customers turned their attention to Al.

"Runyan, you're a little boy to be fighting a war," one man shouted above the commotion of laughter. "You stay in Pueblo and protect the home folks."

"Yeah, someone's got to write stories about us when we get all shot up," another said, "and you're just the boy."

Voices came from all parts of the bar.

"You can tell them about the medals we win."

"Runyan, you can keep the beer cold for us while we're away."

"Yeah, and the girls warm."

"We'll tell you all about it when we get back."

Al's face was pale and menacing. "I'll be there to-morrow," he said, moving his eyes along the groups of faces to see if anyone would contradict him, "and I'll be marching away with you."

But Al didn't appear at the recruiting station the next day. Afraid the army would reject him because of his age if he attempted to enlist in Colorado, he was on his way to Minnesota, where he joined the 13th Minnesota

Volunteers. He had run away from his age in order to become a soldier.

Although the army did most of its fighting against Spain in Cuba, the wartime destiny of Al Runyan, and most of the volunteers from the western states, was fashioned 7000 miles to the west in the Philippine Islands. On May 1, Commodore George Dewey's Asiatic Squadron captured Manila Bay, destroying or disabling the entire Spanish fleet. This great naval victory gave Dewey, who was immediately named an admiral, and the American government, an unusual problem. The Spanish commander in Manila was willing to surrender the city to the American fleet, but Dewey would not hear of this because he did not have enough men to hold and police the city. The situation was further complicated by the Philippine insurgents who had been at war with the Spanish since 1896. General Emilio Aguinaldo, commander of the native insurgents, had declared himself dictator-president of the Philippine Republic, and had a large army ready to advance on Manila.

He was willing to cooperate with Dewey, but apparently America was not fighting the war to free the Philippines for the natives. The men in Washington, reasoning that it was ridiculous to win the race and not eat the pie, issued orders for the organization of a Philippine expeditionary force. The American plan soon became clear; we would first conquer the Philippines with our own forces, then decide later what we would do with the islands.

General Wesley Merritt, who had been named commander of the expeditionary force to the Philippines, established his headquarters in San Francisco. He requested 14,000 men for his army, pleading that the greater portion of these troops be regular army men with military experience under their belts rather than patriotic glory bubbling in their hearts. General Merritt received Al Runyan and a host of other volunteers, all of whom were improperly equipped, lacking articles of ordnance, tents, and light clothing. But they were brave, strong men, Al Runyan and the rest of them, as they marched through the streets of San Francisco on their way to the docks and the transports.

"Every street leading from the Presidio to the Pacific Mail dock, a distance of about five miles, was lined with people," one account of the march read. "At Vanness Avenue the entire police force of San Francisco was waiting and fell in ahead of the soldiers. There was one continuing roar of cheers, flags were waved frantically. . . . Nothing like the sight on Market Street was ever seen here before. Many weeping women followed along after the soldiers. As the marching men neared the waterfront bombs were fired, steam whistles blown, and every device imaginable for making noise was put into full operation."

On May 25, at 5 P.M., three ships, carrying the first American expeditionary force to leave the western hemisphere, sailed out of San Francisco and into the Pacific. When the American troops disembarked in the Philippines, they were ordered into entrenched positions near Pasay, three miles south of Manila. The soldiers looked toward the ancient city and took notice of the strange land around them: the rich foliage, laced with bamboo stalks, hiding the swamps; the clear, flat patches of rice fields; and the rising pattern of causeways, where the packed dirt roads led to the city.

Al dropped his rifle to his side, encircling its barrel with thumb and forefinger. The high hills, warmed by the sun and lightly touched by the blue sky, was a new beauty, different from the imperial mountains that sweep into Colorado from the Rockies. The dark shadows on the slopes, leading to the valleys, were deep, opaque, mysterious with imagined terrors. It made Al lonely for the Home Café, for the soft look of a Pueblo girl. But nearer, where the land ran down, along, and up to his boots, all was shabby and the grass was bent and gray with dust. A bullet voiced its strength in the air above Al's head. He awakened, startled, and then noticed that the trenches in the distance were filled with Spaniards. Al quickly sought out a protective barrier.

Meanwhile, plans for the surrender of Manila were being arranged. General Jaudenes, interested in preserving some of the Spanish military honor, said he could not surrender the city unless the Americans made an attack. But he not only promised that the Manila shore batteries would hold their fire, but said arrangements had been made for the Spanish troops to retreat in good order, firing over the heads of the advancing Americans. Both Admiral Dewey and General Merritt were pleased with this plan, for it would be a bloodless battle, and General Aguinaldo's insurgents could be kept out of the city. Admiral Dewey's ships would fire a few rounds in the general direction of the city, and the American troops would advance slowly on Manila, giving the Spaniards time to retreat.

The battle began on August 13, at 9 A.M., when Dewey's fleet opened fire, and the American troops moved forward toward Manila. But the engagement did not come off exactly as it had been rehearsed in the minds of the American and Spanish commanders. A tropical rainstorm rolled in over the troops, making it difficult for the advancing units to keep in contact with one another. When the native troops in the area saw the Americans moving into battle, they rushed forward, too. The insurgent army had no intention of being left out of the capture of Manila. On one narrow road leading through the rice fields to the city, large bands of rebels crowded in with the American troops. There wasn't room for both contingents, and the advancing warriors had to elbow each other aside as they marched along.

The insurgents, and some of the Americans who carried glory in their hearts and a hatred for the nefarious Spaniards who had blown up the *Maine*, were shooting to kill. This made the Spaniards do some shooting of their own, and several animated skirmishes ensued. When the battle reached the city walls, it was difficult to distinguish the retreating Spaniards from the advancing Americans and insurgents. Troops of various sizes, shapes, and allegiances came hurrying from unexpected directions. Somehow, in the confusion, the Americans captured the city, and at the same time were able to keep most of the Filipinos outside Manila.

While the troops were marching toward Manila, the 1st Colorado Regiment band followed along the beach playing "There'll Be a Hot Time in the Old Town Tonight." The idea of a band playing while a soldier marched to battle fascinated Al. As the music continued, Al trudged along singing the chorus:

"Please, oh, please, oh, do not let me fall;
  You're all mine, and I love you best of all;
  You must be my man or I'll have no man at all—
  There'll be a hot time in the old town tonight!"

Al never forgot the band marching along the beach that summer morning when Manila fell. It was one of the high points of the war for him.

"We had a band," he wrote many years later, when he gave his account of the battle.

"Yes, sir, a band.

"Off to the left of the advancing lines, right behind the skirmishers, it marched on Manila, one of the spare bandsmen lugging an American flag and another toting the regimental colors of the 1st Colorado Volunteers to which the band belonged.

"Yes, sir, and it played:

" 'When you hear them bells go ting-ga-ling

" 'Oompah, oompah, oompah.'

"I have forgotten how many men it took to make a regimental band in those days. Maybe thirty, forty. The bandsmen were supposed to double as litter bearers in a pinch. I have no idea how the 1st Colorado bandsmen came to go into action with their musical instruments, but the leader was a kind of a big man back home and maybe that had something to do with it.

"Anyway, there they were, marching along and there was something comforting in the familiar strains that they sent floating across the muddy rice paddies on that misty morning:

" 'All join hands and sweetly we will sing—

" 'Oompah, oompah, oompah.'

"The long-barreled breech-loading Springfields of the volunteers, the men from Pennsylvania, Colorado, Minnesota, Montana, Utah, Oregon and other states gave out smoky roars. The Krag-Jörgensens of the regulars spoke more sharply. Now and then the little mountain guns of the Astor Battery under the dashing Peyton March went blup-blup, blup, blup and all the time the band shrilled:

" 'When the verse am through the chorus all join in—

" 'Oompah, oompah, oompah.'

"Ah, yes, it was a little war, but it was such a brave little war, with a handful of rank greenhorns 10,000 miles from a base marching behind a band in a battle that was to take an empire.

"Occasionally a man in the advancing lines pitched forward on his face and lay quite still. The dead never know the size of a war. The route over which the band was moving took it along the beach. The tide was coming in and the musicians splashed water high above their leggings as they tried to keep step to their own music.

" 'There'll be a hot time in the old town tonight—

" 'Oompah, oompah, oompah.'

"Later when the yellow and gold flag of old Spain came down over Fort Malate and the walled town and everywhere else in the Pacific and the Stars and Stripes rose in its place, the tired volunteers and regulars marched into the city and sprawled on the cobbled roads to rest their weary bones while their outfits were assigned to stations.

"The people had been only mildly enthusiastic over their arrival and stood around eyeing them curiously until down the Escolta came that same band of the 1st Colorado apparently as fresh as ever and playing:

" 'There'll be a hot time in the old town tonight—
     My Baby—

" 'Oompah, oompah, oompah.'

"The people clapped and cheered.

"The soldiers sang for them the words of the song that was for years afterwards the song of the islands. The band kept going:

" 'Oompah, oompah, oompah.' "

As soon as Al arrived in Manila he began reconnoitering the lay of the land. What angles could be exploited? How could army life be made more tolerable? With what divining rod could a resourceful man tap the wellsprings of pleasure in this island? Al's mind began searching for the answers. He saw no reason for calling a moratorium on the pursuit of happiness because he was engaged in a war. Al moved through the city like a curious sightseer.. A group of soldiers came tramping through the city gate. It was the Colorado regiment. Al had been waiting for them, and now he examined their columns closely until he found the contingent from Pueblo.

"Hey, you cow-bellied shirkers from Pueblo," Al yelled, thumbing his nose in their direction. "Hey, over here you club-footed soldiers."

When the Pueblo boys recognized Al waving in the street, they all returned his five-fingered salute.

"Hey, I told you guys the Minnesota regiment had a mascot," Joe yelled, pointing to Al. "There he is. Ugly animal, ain't he?"

Al walked with the troops as they plodded along the streets of Manila. "Where have you rubbernecks been?" he asked. "Fighting a rear-guard action in the bushes? The band did more fighting than you guys."

"Go on, show us how brave you are," Bill sneered. "Smoke a cigarette right here in the middle of the street."

But the boys from Colorado had the last laugh. They were quartered in a palatial Spanish home, which the army had commandeered for use as a barracks. Al could not disguise his envy when he learned that his erstwhile comrades were practically living in the lap of luxury.

Al had made a practice of developing a few friends in the right places, reasoning that there might be occasions when these associations would come in handy. This was such an occasion. One day about a week later, Al appeared in the barracks of the Colorado regiment carrying his gun and inquiring for the officer-in-charge. A Filipino boy, who had attached himself to Al and acted as his personal messenger, body servant, and all-around lackey, followed close behind him. The Filipino was carrying Al's pack and all his personal gear. The Pueblo boys crowded around the pair.

"Where the hell are you going, Runyan?" Joe asked. "Taking an overnight hike into the hills?"

"I've come here to stay."

The Colorado group stared at him skeptically, half expecting a trick. They demanded an explanation.

"You're what?"

"I'm going to live here, make my dwelling here, reside here, enhance this pigsty with my presence. What's the matter with you guys, have you forgotten the English language already?"

"You mean you're going to bunk here?"

"Exactly. I always wanted to live in a Spanish castle, or a reasonable facsimile."

"How did you manage this?" Joe asked.

"It's very simple if you have friends in the higher echelon," Al explained. "It's all done with a bit of behind-the-scenes manuevering. But you lame brains wouldn't understand this."

"We understand it all right," Joe said, "but we have another name for it."

Al stared at Joe for a moment, trying to discover any sign of unfriendliness in his remark.

"You know, Joe," Al said, finally, "you've got to be careful how you talk to me from now on. My little friend here is very sensitive."

The group turned to the Filipino as though they were noticing him for the first time. The native boy smiled at them, unembarrassed, showing his even white teeth. The Pueblo boys studied him carefully, and then sent another stream of questions at Al.

"What's this kid doing here?"

"He's my retinue."

"Your what?"

"My man Friday."

"You mean he's your slave."

"Now, gentlemen, let's be polite about this," Al said,

patting the Filipino on the head. "This boy is my friend and helper. I raised him from a pup."

"Leave it to Al," Tom remarked, and all the Pueblo boys nodded their heads in agreement and wonder.

Al's bunk was near a window, facing the road. One day the Colorado boys found him sitting on the edge of his cot holding a long pipe in his mouth. Every few minutes he would pull the pipe from his mouth and duck his head below the window.

"What the hell are you up to now, Runyan?" Joe inquired. "Are you taking up some native religion?"

"This is a blow pipe," Al replied mildly, handing it to the group for their inspection. "The natives blow feather darts through it, and use it for a weapon. Some of them can hit an ant at fifty yards."

"So the army won't trust you with a gun," Bill remarked, holding the pipe up to the light as though inspecting it. "Have to fight the war with a blow pipe."

"The blow pipe has many uses," Al said, ignoring the insult. "Watch this."

He took a small clay pellet, which had been carefully packed with mineral matter, and dropped it into the tube of the pipe. Then, putting the pipe in his mouth, he peered out the window.

"Look for a target," he instructed the group.

Before long a native girl, walking with carefree and leisurely steps, came into view. When she stopped in front of the window to smile at a soldier on the other side of the street, Al blew. There was a piercing scream as the native girl leaped into the air like a chicken that has lost its dignity. The girl rubbed her buttock, and turned toward the window. Her eyes, round and black, glared savagely. The boys waved and shouted words of fondness to her, but the girl stuck out her tongue at them and ran down the road.

"Well, Al, you queered a good time for that guy across the street," Bill said, slapping him on the back.

"Hey, Runyan," Joe said, "you certainly won't be able to do much wooing around here if you keep that up."

Al rose to his feet and turned to the group. "Gentlemen," he began quietly, "let me inform you of the purpose of this delicate, efficient little instrument. It is true that a soldier can never talk back to an officer. Right?"

"As true as the button on your belly," someone remarked.

"When we joined the army we lost our constitutional right of free speech. . . ."

"Hey, Al, you'd better hide that pipe," Tom cautioned. "The lieutenant's coming up the road."

Al returned to the window. "Now I'll give you a demonstration of how you can regain your freedom of speech," he said, placing a clay pellet in the blow pipe, and crouching at the window, with just his head appearing above the sill. He took careful aim, and when the lieutenant stepped into the proper target angle, his blue uniform outlined against the sun, Al blew on the pipe. The lieutenant jumped a few inches off the ground, and then wheeled around, his face red with anger, his hands grasping his buttocks.

"Looks like you scared him for life, Runyan," Joe said, as the group scrambled away from the window.

"I was merely preserving my constitutional rights," Al

observed, hiding the pipe under a loose board in the floor.

One by one the boys from Pueblo came over to Al, shook his hand, and then hurried out of the barracks in order to be out of sight when the lieutenant came in. They were glad that Al was one of the gang again.

Al resumed his newspaper career as a part-time reporter for the service paper in Manila, and also began some experiments in writing verse. He wrote for the *Manila Freedom,* the soldier's paper, *The Soldier's Letter,* an illustrated monthly magazine devoted to the United States Army and Navy at Manila, and the *Souvenir Song Book,* a small volume containing twenty-five original songs and poems written by members of the Eighth Army Corps. Some of the Pueblo boys began kidding him about his poetry.

He was resting on his cot one day, a pad propped up on his knees, a pencil in his hand, his mind working to compose a poem, when he noticed Joe approaching. Joe carried one of his hands on his hip, and he waved the other hand lightly in the air before him as though he were picking butterflies from a rosebush.

"Mr. Runyan, I understand you are a poet," he said in a singing falsetto voice. "I think that's just too wonderful. I'd just love to read some of your poems, but I'll be back this evening when we can be alone."

"Hey, leatherhead, come back here," Al yelled, as Joe started to dance away. "I'm going to make you read some of my verses. You're one of those crawling apes who thinks he's a man because he can grow a beard and only knows how to curse when this Army gets him down. I don't pretend to be a poet. I'm only a sort of bush-league Kipling. But I do know that there are some things you can't say unless you write a poem. That way, at least I can give my curses some meaning."

Al reached under his cot and pulled a piece of paper out of an envelope. "Do you have any trouble with your uniforms, Joe?" Al asked, handing him the paper. "Take a look at this."

Joe sat down on the edge of the cot and read:

> I'm a-comin' up from stables in me ragged pantaloons
>   An' me shirt tail's flyin' freely out behind;
> An' me ridin' seat has patchin's grinnin' like a pair o'
>   moons—
>   'Tis a job I did me ownself, d'ye mind.
> An' I hears the sergeant bawl: "Hi, come to th' barrack
>   hall;
>   All th' officers is lookin' you askance.
> Yer clothes they is a sight, an' th' fittin' is a fright—
>   Come on an' git some pants, pants, pants!"

"Yeah, Al, I see what you mean," Joe said, returning the verse. "I guess I've been a dope riding you about it. What's that one you're working on now?"

Al gave him the pad. "I call it 'Hoof Beats.' I got a few more verses to go on it," he said.

> What do the horses' hoofses say
>   Poundin' on the road?
> Raisin' a blanket o' dusty gray,
>   Complainin' o' their load?
> Listen, an' hear 'em talk—
> Gallop or trot or walk,
>   This is what the hoofses say
>   Poundin' on the road:

"A mile! A mile! A mile!"
Boot 'em along an' smile!
The sabers clank to the plankety-plank—
"A mile! A mile! A mile!"

What do the horses' hoofses say?
  To some o' home they speaks—
See 'em dreamin' the miles away
  An' many a smile they sneaks.
Friends an' a people dear,
Many a mile from here;
  To them the horses' hoofses say
  Poundin' on the road:

"A mile! A mile! A mile!"
We'll get home after awhile:
Me, Oh, my! The road slides by—
"A mile! A mile! A mile!"

One of Al's most disturbing war experiences was his short turn of duty in the signal corps. He was assigned to a balloon detail which made a daily scouting flight, drifting above the treetops, noting the nature of the terrain, and observing the positions of the insurgent army. The native riflemen, who believed that the balloon might be a machination of the devil, but, in any case, was not doing their cause any good, fired a few rounds at the floating gas bag every time it came in sight.

The insurgents who were in control of the Philippine islands of Luzon, Negros, Cebu, and Panay were becoming restless, and their hostility to the Americans grew stronger each day our troops remained in Manila. The Spanish-American War ended on August 12, 1898, and in the peace treaty the United States agreed to pay Spain $20,000,000 for the Philippine Archipelago. When General Aguinaldo learned that the United States intended to take over the entire area of the Philippines, he was more than a little perturbed.

At 8:30 P.M., on February 4, 1899, the inevitable happened. An insurgent patrol of four men crossed a bridge that led into American territory on the northern border of Manila. A Nebraska volunteer on sentry duty challenged the Filipinos and ordered them to retreat. When the natives continued to advance the sentry fired at them, and the Philippine War began. In the first four days of fighting 268 Americans were killed or wounded, and more than 500 Filipinos were dead. Before this war ended two years later, it cost the United States as much in life and effort as did the entire Spanish-American War. The Philippine expeditionary force had finally found its war, 7000 miles from home.

Al was wounded twice—once at the Battle of Inmus, and again at Samar—but neither injury was serious. It was difficult for him to be frivolous about this war, for he understood the fever and the dread that pulsed through all his comrades. He wrote a poem called "Going and Coming," and when the boys from Pueblo read it, they understood what he had meant when he defended writing poetry.

When we went to Marishoa, warn't we feelin' gay,
Slippin' 'long th' dusty road an' singin' on th' way;
When we went to Marishoa, warn't we feelin' fine—
Eighty hoss, two hundred foot an' field guns in th' line:

(Marishoa is up a hill—
Marishoa is up there still—)
'Ray! We went to Marishoa feelin' pretty fine!

When we came from Marishoa, bringin' o' our dead,
Heads a-hangin' heavy an' our hearts as chunks o' lead;
When we come from Marishoa, not a song wuz heard—
Not a smilin' face we brought, not a cheerin' word—
(Marishoa is up a hill—
Marishoa is up there still—)
An' we left 'em layin' there with th' Chaplain's Word!

And again in a poem called "Veteran and Recruit," he said:

We are goin' into action, as we've often gone before;
An' we know our blasted feelin's like a book;
A hundred times, perhaps, we heard this same old battleroar
An' these shakin's we're a-shakin' always shook.
Oh, we're goin' into battle, you kin hear our molars rattle;
For veteran or rooky, it's th' same;
But you mustn't ever show it; ever let th' fellers know it;
An' when you die they'll mention you went game!

Al was with the American troops who were bivouacked at Guiguinto, a village near Malalos, the capital of the Filipino Republic. It was here that he began holding hands with a pretty native girl named Anastacia Bailerino. He was fond of most of the native girls and boasted that a Sulu girl named Laloa, who lived on an island Al called the "Isle of Content," was the mother of his son and heir. Joe became impatient with this tale of Laloa and her son.

"Listen, Runyan," he said one day, "you don't know a Sulu girl, or a girl name Lalao on this whole God-damned island. That baby, just like your manhood, is all in your head."

But Al knew Anastacia.

"Her eyes are black, her hair is as a raven's wing," Al said, reciting the charms of his loved one, "and her lips are rosy red, which is not surprising considering the way she chews betel nuts."

Anastacia lived with her parents in a little thatched hut which was set up on stilts a good pole-vaulter's jump from the ground. Al was a frequent visitor at the Bailerino straw house. He considered the fact that the house was raised off the ground very accommodating, since it provided him with a shady spot to conduct his wooing of Anastacia. The courtship progressed nicely despite the fact that Anastacia owned not only a pig named Otis, but a pet python she called Alexander. The python had a habit of peering under the house occasionally, usually from some unexpected corner, and at the most inopportune moments. Al was on very friendly terms with Otis, however, and the pig frequently followed him back to camp.

Meanwhile, the troops at camp were considerably disturbed over the fact that in a continuing series of meals they had been served nothing but beans. A committee was formed to bring the soldiers' grievance before the company cook, a man named Skillman.

"It isn't that we mind having beans every day," one of the members of the committee said, "but we can't remember that our mothers had such consistent bad luck with their beans as you do with yours, Skillman."

Skillman had his defense ready. "I agree that what you say is true," the cook commented, "but let me remind you that your mother had something to put in her beans that

I don't have—pork. Get it—pork, pork, pork. It makes all the difference in the world."

All eyes turned to Al. "You heard what he said, Runyan," a committee member remarked. "Skillman said the beans need pork. Pork like you get from pigs."

The following day the troops at Guiguinto had pork and beans for dinner. The soldiers could hardly contain themselves after this feast, and the news that pork and beans had been served at camp spread for miles around. The next time Al went to call on Anastacia he was greeted by the sound of a bullet screaming over his head. He quickly learned that Anastacia considered it more than a happy coincidence that the boys in camp enjoyed pork with their beans the same day Otis disappeared. From that time on she was only on shooting terms with him.

Al was fascinated by the leisurely and uninhibited life of the natives, especially the freedom from convention and ignorance of culture enjoyed by the males. But after a time the habits of some of them became annoying, and for the troops who had to fight to secure the Philippines, the decision of the United States to take up the White Man's burden in Asia was even more irritating. Al expressed the sentiment of the men when he wrote a poem about the Mohammedan Malays who live in the southern Philippines and are known as Moro men.

Th' Moro is a cur'ous bug, a cur'ous bug is he;
He builds his house on little stilts out o' a bamboo tree;
An' when he's tired o' livin' there an' wants ter move his shack,
He makes his wife put down her wash an' moves it on her
    back!

Chorus:

But you mustn't hurt th' Moro, boys,
        Or take away his gun,
For if you do you'll surely hear
        From 'em at Washington.
You mustn't hurt th' Moro, boys,
        He's jes' a little wild.
Oh, treat th' Moro gently, boys!
        He's Uncle Sammy's child!

Th' Moro is a cheerful cuss; he never works at all;
He sits an' smokes a cigarette from springtime into fall;
He ain't so fond o' cleanliness—he ruther likes th' dirt—
An' all th' clo'es he has ter wear is jes' a little shirt!

Th' Moro is a peaceful cuss; he never likes to fight—
"Barai!" is th' Moro's word from mornin' until night.
He likes ter take a shot at us, but jes' for practice' sake—
Oh, do not hurt th' Moro, boys; you might keep him awake!

Th' Moro is a funny cuss, for when we gits our pay
He sells us anything he's got—an' steals it right away.
He pots us from th' underbrush or whacks us with a knife—
But you mustn't hurt th' Moro, boys, his children, or his wife!

Th' Moro is a friendly cuss; it's jes' his little way
Ter shoot at us through half th' night—an' ginurly all day;
We catch him after chasin' him until we a'most faint;
He's friendly then till next day when—th' chances is he ain't!

Chorus:

Oh, do not hurt th' Moro, boys;
        He's Uncle Sammy's child;

> An' when you speak be sure your tones
>   Are soft an' low an' mild;
> Oh, do not mind his knife, my boys;
>   He's jes' a little riled;
> An' do not hurt th' Moro, boys—
>   He's Uncle Sammy's child!

In the fall of 1899, Al was shipped to China for a short period of duty training American and Chinese recruits near Peking, and in December his company received their long-awaited orders to return to the United States. Al was mustered out of the Army in San Francisco. He felt in his pockets and discovered that they were in the same condition as when he enlisted—empty. He returned to Pueblo by the same method of transportation he had used when he left—hitch-hiking.

4

COMING AND GOING

When Al returned to Pueblo, he found a change in his
father; the old man had grown old. He had slowed down
the tempo of his walk, stopped carrying his shoulders stiff
and straight like a drill master's, and spent less time touch-
ing up his goatee and mustache. He let the gray hairs crop
out where they pleased, threw away his starched collars,
and neglected to shine his shoes. One afternoon Al and
his father had a drink and a quiet talk in the room at the
Mount Pleasant. Old man Runyan admitted that his life
had changed while Al was away.

"Yes, sir, you can call me your old man now and you'll be right," Runyan said, cheerfully. "You know how I first became aware that I was moving into the age of senility? When I started leaving the house half dressed. 'You doddering old cow,' I said to myself. The other day I left the table with loose chewings on my chin, and they would be there yet if someone hadn't called my attention to them. 'Runyan, you emasculated goat,' I said, 'you've got to face facts.'"

"Old man, you're crazy as a loon," Al remarked, laughing easily. "You're not growing old, you're just beginning to take it easy and enjoy life. It's about time."

"Oh, I'm enjoying myself, all right, since I abandoned my practice of reading the obituary notices."

"Obituary notices?"

"Yes, the obituary columns," Runyan continued. "Every time I read of the death of one of my contemporaries, it depressed me no end. I'd consult a doctor, and go on diets, and was worse than an old woman trying to keep her youth. But now I skip the death notices in the paper, eat what I please, and my doctor's bills have been cut by two-thirds."

"I'll believe you're getting old when I find out that you've stopped chasing the women," Al said, pouring his father another drink.

"Oh, I still watch the women to see how the stock is running," Runyan said, rocking in his chair contentedly. "But I hate to run into some of these well-rounded matrons, because I can remember when they were pretty young things. And what a fancy I took to some of them! But now I just look at them and I know my age. It's like looking at the teeth of a horse. But the hardest brunt to bear is when I tell a story at the Arkansas Saloon, and one of the spittoon tenders they have for customers says he heard me tell that same story before. I'm getting to be a bore."

Runyan was seized by a fit of coughing. Al noticed that the cough was persistent, hard, and deep in his father's chest.

"I've been coughing like this for a year," Runyan said. "Can't seem to get rid of it."

Neither of the men mentioned the cough again. But both remembered that it was only twelve years ago that Libbie Runyan packed her bags and returned home to Kansas.

Al returned to his newspaper career as a member of the staff of the *Pueblo Chieftain*. He now considered himself an ace reporter, at least in his own home town. The editors apparently agreed with him, and frequently gave him a by-line. One day a printer made a typographical error, and Al's last name appeared in the paper as RUNYON. The mistake pleased Al, and he began signing all his stories with the revised spelling of his name. He sought out the printer who was responsible for the error and took him to the Home Café for a drink.

"I certainly feel it's my duty to buy a drink for the man who volunteered to change my name for the better without any legal paraphernalia, or church services," Al explained to the surprised printer.

Al found no contentment in the security of having a home town, with its friendliness of known places and persons. The quiet comfort that some people experience in understanding their environment gave him no pleasure. He left town frequently to discover what was on the other side of the mountain; he walked, begged rides, and rode the freight trains. People said the war had made Al restless, but the seeds of discontent were planted in him long before the sinking of the *Maine*. They said Al Runyan would never amount to much, always roaming around the country up to goodness knows what. But Al never accepted the preordained precepts of good and evil, truth and error, black and white that had been set before him as the healthy nourishment for a growing boy. He wanted to form his own rules of good and evil—especially evil. In the end, he discovered that, except for cloistered monks, the measure of morality depended on what side of the street you were standing on. Al preferred to observe the type of evil common to gamblers, rumrunners, fixers, assorted second-story men, and all-around wastrels, to that of politicians, business executives, diplomats, storekeepers, stockbrokers, and churchmen.

One day Al found himself strolling down the path leading to the water tank that stood near the railroad tracks on the outskirts of Pueblo. His walking there was more a matter of instinct than an act of will. He didn't fully realize that he had made up his mind to leave town again until a man sitting against one of the stanchions supporting the water tank called to him.

"Taking a trip, Mack?" the man asked, with good-natured friendliness.

Al recognized the man as one of the clan of hoboes who gathered near the railroad water tank because the trains usually stopped there to refill their boilers.

"I guess I am," Al answered, amused at himself. He thought he had been walking aimlessly through town, look-

ing for some excitement, but instead, he had been directing his steps toward the water tank in order to hop an out-
going freight. He had no idea where he wanted to go.

"I knew you weren't a shack," the hobo said. "I could
tell by your face and the way you walked. You go along
nice and easy, like you ain't got no place to go, and you
don't want to hurt nobody. Do you know what a shack is?"

"Yeah, he's one of them railroad bulls, I guess," Al
answered.

"Yeah, they're plenty mean."

Al drew a small knife out of a coat pocket, and began
cutting his initials on one of the stanchions. There was a
line of names embedded in the wood, painted and carved,
as high as Al could reach. He read some of the names to the
hobo: Cincy Skin, Peoria Shine, Cheyenne Red, Reading
Blackie, and A No. 1.

"Say, who belongs to all these queer names?" Al asked.

"Those are all the boys," the hobo answered, coming
over to take a look. "There's my moniker down there."

Al bent down to read the name, freshly cut in the stan-
chion. "Jake the Lean, is that you?" he asked.

"Ha, ha, ha, yeah, that's me, Jake the Lean," the hobo
said proudly. "The water tanks is sort of a hotel register for
the hoboes. See the arrow next to my name? That's to show
which way I'm going case any of my friends come along
this way. See that A No. 1? That's the guy supposed to be
king of us 'boes. But don't pay no attention to that. I say
he's a faker."

The sound of a train approaching, heavy-wheeled, and
soft-whistled, stopped the conversation. Jake the Lean led
the way to a clump of bushes near the track. When the

hobo spotted an open boxcar, he broke through the bushes and ran toward the train, Al following him. Al and the hobo bounded into the boxcar and moved to one of its darkened corners.

"This has always been a good town," Jake the Lean commented, as the men settled down for a long journey. "I don't think we'll be bothered by any shacks."

He then told his story of A No. 1, the so-called King of the Hoboes. Jake the Lean said that A No. 1 had traveled an incredible number of miles on the railroads without paying a single fare and had painted or carved his name on almost every railroad building and shack west of the Mississippi. But old-timers among the hoboes argued that A No. 1 was not even qualified to be a member of their clan.

"And they call him the King," Jake the Lean complained, enumerating some of the rules for the hobo on the road that their monarch had violated. A No. 1 was never known to "hit the stem" (beg on the street). He had a talent for carving a potato into a person's likeness, and it was charged that he accepted pay for his work, an unpardonable sin in Jake the Lean's mind.

"And you know what else he does?" the hobo continued, making no attempt to hide his disgust for the impostor. "I got this from Gypsy Blood. Gypsy Blood told me that A No. 1 was paying the shacks to let him ride the rods. What do you think of that one?"

Al observed paying a shack did not seem to be a very ethical practice for a hobo.

"But I'll say one thing for him," Jake the Lean remarked, willing to give A No. 1 his due. "There's none can beat him making 'em on the fly. Why, he can hop onto a freight moving better than thirty-five miles an hour."

That evening when the train slowed down, Jake the Lean hurried to the door of the car and peered into the dusk. To Al the view was just another obscure, flat piece of landscape; they were probably on the outskirts of some town.

"Looking for a shack, Jake?" he asked nervously.

"No, this is our dinner stop," Jake the Lean said quickly. "Follow me."

The hobo leaped off the train, running along the outer bed of the tracks to keep his balance when he hit the ground. Al jumped, lost his footing on the cinders, and plunged head over heels down the embankment into a wire fence.

"Like jumping into a deep well, eh, son?" the hobo said, helping Al to his feet. "Take's a little time to learn the tricks."

Jake the Lean led the way through a cluster of woods to a clearing near a creek, where several hoboes were huddled around a fire. This was a "jungle," one of the hobo camps that can be found near the railroad in almost any town. The men were so busy eating stew out of the tin cans they held pinched between their knees, they glanced only once at the newcomers.

One of the hoboes threw two empty tin cans over near the fire.

"Help yourselves," he said.

Al and Jake the Lean picked up the cans and dipped them cautiously into the stew bubbling in the black, dented pot hanging over the fire. Then they took their places in

the circle. Al noticed the solitary figure of a man bent over
a small fire near the edge of the river bank. At regular
intervals, he studiously skimmed something off the top of
the broth.

"What's the matter with that guy, is he a snob?" Al
asked. "Or does he think it's unhealthy to eat from a community pot."

"No, that's a John Yegg," Jake the Lean answered in a
low, respectful whisper. "A John Yegg is a real tough guy
. . . blows up safes. . . . He's boiling dynamite, and that
stuff he's skimming off is the nitro. That's the stuff that
makes the big boom. I guess he's going to blow a safe
tonight."

After the circle had finished the stew, refilling their cans
several times with the rich mixture in the pot, Al passed
around a pack of cigarettes. Each of the hoboes lighted
one, puffing on it carefully, almost reverently. Then they
began to tell stories, speaking in hushed, awed tones about
their great enemy, the railroad shack, the only real evil in
the world. The hoboes agreed that the toughest shack in
the country once rode the freight trains of the Santa Fe
railroad running between Dodge City, Kansas, and La
Junta, Colorado. When this shack spotted a hobo riding
the rods, he would climb to the top of the boxcar and wait
until the train was coursing at full speed. Then he would
attach a coupling pin to a long wire, and drop the pin to
the ground, securing the wire to the top of the boxcar. The
pin would bounce under the car with devastating force,
slashing relentlessly at the unfortunate hobo until he was
finally unseated from his precarious berth.

Al could sense the hoboes shivering. They seemed like

haunted shadows in the firelight, remembering the fate of many of their friends. A bottle of whiskey passed from hand to hand. Al knew it was bad liquor, but he took a big swig from the bottle. Jake the Lean laughed.

"How about what a John Yegg did to that shack?" he said.

"Yeah, what about that shack, tell us the story, tell us the story," the others chorused. They all knew the story, but they wanted to hear it again.

"One day that shack found a John Yegg riding the rods," Jake the Lean began, and the circle of hoboes listened, with soft smiles on their faces. "He gets on top of the boxcar, and starts giving John Yegg the business with the pin, and John Yegg is bruised and cut up so much he falls on the tracks. And the shack thinks he's dead. But John Yegg ain't dead, and no one knows why. When John Yegg recovers from the bruises he goes to work and boils up some dynamite, and pours the nitro soup in a bottle, and he puts the bottle into his hip pocket."

"He's got a surprise for that shack right in his hip pocket," one of the hoboes remarked, unable to restrain himself. Jake the Lean frowned at the interruption, and continued.

"John Yegg goes on the hunt for this shack, and one day he finds him riding on top of a long freight. John Yegg makes the train on the fly and climbs to the top of the boxcar. And the shack starts chasing him, and John Yegg starts a-running along the cars. And John Yegg stops right on the edge of a car, turns his back on the shack, and leans over. That shack takes a good boot and sure enough kicks the bottle in John Yegg's pocket. And before you know it there is the shack and John Yegg flying in the sky higher than the birds. People all around heard the explosion."

The tale was ended, and the hoboes, their optimism and good humor restored, laughed and laughed. Their shrill, crackling voices ascending from the campfire became an eerie, almost inhuman, sound in the night. Al took another drink. It tasted better the second time. He had developed into a formidable drinker, and in this activity the hoboes were willing companions. Liquor was the equation that made desires equal to present possessions; it had a full Christian name, John Barleycorn.

"John Barleycorn, John Barleycorn!"—this was the hoboes' prayer, and their devil. But a hangover for a hobo could be particularly ominous. Although he never joined the clan of tramps, Al knew the meaning of riding the rails with John Barleycorn, and he wrote a poem to commemorate this experience.

I'm roostin' here like a Shantycleer on a rod the size of a match,
With an open view on either side, an' a box-car floor fer a
    thatch.
An' I hope the shack don't find me, fer me face is all he could
    punch,
As I'm beatin' me old friend Vanderbilt an' eatin' his ballast
    fer lunch.
    Oh, the ground slips by like a river,
    An' me nerves are all a-quiver—
Fer I've bin out on a sort o' a bat, an' the rail-points sing to me:
    "John Barleycorn! John Barleycorn!
    John Barleycorn! John Barleycorn!"

Al sympathized with the stubborn, insistent desire of

the hoboes to wander where they pleased, free, without responsibility or purpose, giving to no man, code of laws, or precepts of society their allegiance. They went to extreme lengths to preserve their freedom, but Al sometimes believed that the spirit of the heart was best served in aimless roaming, experiencing the unplanned, the spontaneous, the things that just happen.

Al's roaming was not altogether aimless; he was seeking a future, but now it was obscure and undefined in his mind. When he found a new town that pleased his fancy for something new and hopeful, he went to work for one of the local newspapers. He stayed long enough to realize that his new environment was no better than Pueblo, always leaving on the first day he understood, with something of a shock, that this new, hopeful town was the last place in the world he wanted to be at the moment.

After 1902, Al seldom returned to Pueblo. He had finally broken the cord. One job followed another as he moved through Colorado, from town to town, from paper to paper. Sometimes the line of his career would vanish for a time, erupting in unexpected places. Al was working in San Francisco as a reporter when, on April 18, 1906, at 5:13 A.M., the most violent earthquake in America's history shook the city, killing hundreds of people in their sleep, injuring thousands, and leaving 200,000 homeless. Al went into the streets to help in the rescue work and did what he could to fight the cholera epidemic that followed the earthquake and fire.

Sometime in 1907 Runyon arrived in Denver, Colorado. Here he worked for the *Denver News*, the *Denver Republic*, and the *Denver Post*, and for the first time saw his career forming into a definite pattern. The Denver newspapers, which were both progressive and professional, had become the cradling place for many of the West's talented young writers.

Joe Ward, who was editor of the *Denver Post,* was equal to Colonel McKinney in voicing his discontent with the work of his reporters. When Al began introducing a quaint, homespun tone into some of his stories, Ward, who liked his reporting straight from the shoulder, was quick to call it to his attention.

"Come, come, Runyon," he admonished, "kindly eliminate this aroma of new-mown hay, this note of 'Good evening, neighbor.' I have looked up your record and find you were a messenger in the red-light district of Pueblo most of your youth and I fear you have acquired a worldliness that unfits you for playing the joskin in the large city."

One day the *Post* was scooped by a rival Denver newspaper, and Al, who had been covering the same story for his paper, received a severe scolding. The facts in the opposition's account were negligible, but the story made lively and colorful reading.

"Mr. Ward, that story is a fake," Al attempted to explain.

"It's a good story," Ward replied bluntly.

"Yes, sir, I know it's a good story, but it's an out-and-out fake."

"Mr. Runyon," Ward whispered, "couldn't we have some of those good story fakes now and then?"

The Denver Press Club, where the reporters gathered to drink, play billiards, and gamble at poker, was one of the most active newspaper clubs in the country at the time.

Al was almost a daily visitor at the club, where he was a part of a group of reporters who later found their own prominence as writers, editors, and politicians in New York, Hollywood, and Washington. Among the Press Club members were Gene Fowler, newspaperman, author, and biographer; George Creel, magazine writer, who once ran for governor of California as the Democratic candidate; Tim Healy, who became a political writer for the Hearst press, and later a California lawyer; Al Burch, executive of the *Denver Post*; Burns Mantle, the late theater critic; Arthur T. Chapman, writer and columnist; George C. Hull, magazine and film writer; William MacLeod Rains, writer and war correspondent; Edward Keating, who served a term in Congress, and became an editor for labor newspapers. Runyon also met Charles Van Loan, a short-story writer, who asked Al to furnish him with plots for some of his stories.

Runyon's enthusiasm for sports, which could not be satisfied as a reporter, found expression in various enterprises. He was president of the Colorado State Baseball League for a time, managed a semi-professional baseball team, and promoted boxing matches.

His newspaper stories, written in a fresh, fluid style, were receiving by-lines, and he was also building a definite reader audience.

One evening in 1908 he was sitting at his desk staring into space, his eyes fixed on a soiled ring of dampness on the ceiling, his mind shifting phrases, hunting for the right word, trying to form the lead of his story. A copy boy came up to his desk.

"Boss wants to see you, Mr. Runyon."

Al frowned. The half-formed sentences faded from his mind; he had lost the thread.

"Damn it, I can't do two things at once," Al said. "Tell him I'll be in as soon as I finish this story."

The copy boy insisted. "Boss says you should come in right away. There's some big shot in his office. Some guy all dressed up like he was a bank president or something."

Al grimaced. Another front-office job, or maybe a complaint. "I hope it's a complaint," Al mused as he walked through the office, "it'll be more fun. I've got a defense for every one of my stories for the past two weeks."

Al was introduced to the well-dressed man in the front office. He was Henry L. Doherty, the utilities magnate. Al bit his lip. "What's this all about?" he wondered.

"I am very pleased to meet you," Mr. Doherty said, shaking Al's hand. "I've been hearing a lot about you, son. I hear that you're going to be a great writer some day, and that right now you're one of the smartest and ablest reporters in Denver."

Al shifted his feet.

"Son," Mr. Doherty continued, "I'm here to offer you a job. It's nothing permanent, just something temporary, you understand. I've already talked it over with your employer and he has agreed to grant you a leave of absence if you decide to accept my proposition."

Al coughed quietly. "Yes, sir," he said.

"We electric-light men back in the East are holding a convention next month," Mr. Doherty said. "And we need someone with writing ability, good imagination, and initiative to handle a publicity campaign for us. From what we have read of your newspaper stories, and from what we have heard about you, we have decided that you are the man we want to do the job."

"I've never done anything along these lines before," Al remarked cautiously.

"I'll give you a few days to think it over," Mr. Doherty said, putting on his hat. "Remember if you take the job it'll give you a chance to see New York, the big city."

Al was silent for a moment. "Before you go, Mr. Doherty," he said, in a definite, clear voice, "when would you like me to be in New York?"

It took Al a half hour to write his lead for the story that night. He had just been called a great reporter; people were reading his stuff, knew who he was, remembered his name. Well, that's what the man said. He was going to New York for the first time. He wondered why he had never considered going there before.

Perhaps the desire to go to New York was never born in a person unless his ambition became as big as the city itself. Tonight, Al knew he wanted to take a look at New York. Perhaps he had wanted to go there all along, but just couldn't find the right train.

Al wasn't in New York long before he knew that one day it would be a part of him; this was a place a man could call home, and never become the weary slave of conventional routines. Al did not investigate the Statue of Liberty, the museums, or the public library, but he found Broadway, the shows, and the cafés. The utility men were pleased with his work, and he was happy writing publicity stories that placed these electric-light men among the great benefactors of mankind. He also discovered that liquor under these conditions served to heighten the pleasures already created for you—expanded a joy that already existed in your heart.

Women were wearing peek-a-boo shirtwaists, dotted veils and "Merry Widow" hats, with wide brims and often with birds' nests on top. The old *Life* magazine took notice of the new hats and reported, "Ten gorgeous little father birds were killed to trim the hat with; ten somber little mother birds were left sitting on their nests with nobody to feed them—and the hat was called the Merry Widow." The tight-fitting sheath gown, designed to bring a woman's form and her dress together without unnecessary impediments, was imported from Paris. Viewing the new dress with considerable alarm, the Haute Ton Whist and Literary Club of South Norwalk, Connecticut, resolved "that the sheath gown was but one big step backward toward the fig-leaf," and voted that "the sheath gown is both immodest and homely and this club will do everything in its power to put it down."

In the taverns and cafés the entertainers were singing "Sunbonnet Sue," "That's What the Rose Said to Me," "The Bird on Nellie's Hat," "Red Wing," "I Hear You Calling Me," and "Why Did I Pick a Lemon in the Garden of Love?"

On the stage Maude Adams was appearing in "The Jesters"; Ethel Barrymore was playing in "Her Sister"; George Arliss in "The Devil"; James K. Hackett in "The Prisoner of Zenda"; John Drew in "Jack Straw"; Marie Dressler in "The Boy and the Girl"; and George M. Cohan in "The Yankee Prince."

Runyon was delighted with the entire scene. Just living in New York was far more exciting than playing pool in

Pueblo, managing a semi-professional baseball team, or reporting Colorado's violent mining strikes at Cripple Creek, Trinidad, and Walsenburg.

When his job for the utility men was finished, he hated to leave the big city, and the train trip back to Denver seemed long and weary. Although he had been in New York for only a short time, Al was already homesick for Broadway. Several of the passengers in the coach car were feasting on bananas. One boy found the fruit hard to digest and became sick. Al politely refused the bananas offered to him. He might have been better off if he had decided to ride the rods. His attention was attracted to a buxom mother who held her young twins under one arm while she sliced a ham resting on her lap. The ham was for her three older children. Al considered her performance quite a feat. He peered out the window. The landscape, scaling past his vision, wiped away the hopelessness. "Broadway, Broadway, Broadway"—it was a soft, pleasing lullaby in his mind. Runyon had found in Broadway his first real love.

Al stopped in Denver just long enough to absorb the meaning of his new experience and to give himself time to grasp the fact that he was ready for higher adventure. Within a few months he was on his way to San Francisco, where he had accepted an offer to write a sports column for the *San Francisco Post*. This was the first time Runyon had abandoned general news reporting to devote all his time to a specialty.

The San Francisco earthquake was being blamed for destroying much of the city's famous lush and pagan spirit. But the people's deep desire for pleasure had not died in the ruins of Market Street. It had merely undergone a

natural evolutionary process. Pleasure was still their siren
and only the methods of pursuing her had changed. Even
if the period of the Gay Nineties had been the millennium
—and some people were certain that at least for the hours
of darkness the era of heaven on earth had arrived—it
would not have endured very long. Yet, in San Francisco,
"The Paris of the United States," the same evils, like old,
wicked men, continued to prevail. The rich, booming
sounds of the processional that led the patrons of gayety
to their sins had been changed—certainly—but only to a
lower pitch.

The climax and the final act were still the same. A man
could enter a café or music hall, fill himself with the best
foods, the finest wines and liquors, choose his girl for the
night from a large selection of comeliness, lose a fortune at
the gambling wheel, or become engaged in a brawl. How
many women did he need? How much money could he
lose? How many men could a single individual fight? The
preachers in San Francisco would invariably answer, "Too
many," and called the earthquake God's just retribution to
the people for their unrepentant hearts. Not since the days
of the Old Testament, the preachers said, had the inhabitants of one city engaged so wilfully in sin on such a large
scale. No one took the lesson of Sodom seriously. But this
was a modern age, and an earthquake could be explained
by science as an unusual manifestation of nature, not the
work of an angry, omnipotent power.

Runyon did nothing to help the cause of preachers while
he was in San Francisco. One of his closest friends was
David Palter, whom Al called "Little Davey." Together
they made nightly tours of the cafés. Little Davey hunted

for high-stake card games, while Al enjoyed the spectacle of well-dressed men and women attempting to re-create the emotional freedom they knew when they were children splashing in a wading pool. One night Little Davey went broke while engaged in a card game. He hurried to a pawn-broker, pledged a gold watch and chain for a $250 loan, and returned to the game. It continued on until the dawn and then into the bright morning. Al stayed on as an interested, but silent kibitzer. When the game ended at noon, Little Davey had $250,000 in his pockets.

One of Al's friends was "Spider" Kelly, who owned a popular café and employed the most efficient bouncer in San Francisco. The bouncer, who was born in Manassa, Kansas, had come into the city from the hobo trails. He could work with either hand and always had the situation well under control. His name was Jack Dempsey. Kelly, who was a former lightweight boxer, told Runyon that Dempsey might do very well in the ring, and confided that he was teaching him to box. Al advised another good friend, Jack "Doc" Kearns, that Dempsey had all the physical endowments of a first-class fighter. Kearns thought Runyon was right, and later he became Dempsey's manager. Runyon nicknamed Dempsey "The Manassa Mauler."

Al was not always the detached and objective observer during his night prowling. He was ready at all times to defend his own cause with his fists. To celebrate the aggressive powers he displayed in a melee, though hardly to commemorate his nationality, Al was called "The Fighting Irishman." It was in San Francisco that Al began staying up all night, a practice which was to develop into his normal way of life. Many of San Francisco's businessmen made a good living providing the fascinating reasons for remaining awake until dawn. "The Bucket of Blood" was the after hours rendezvous of the "hot sports" of San Francisco.

The Barbary Coast ran from a point south of Market Street to Leavenworth Street, and from Jackson Street over to what is now known as North Beach. At least once a night Al visited The Schiff Bros. Café and the Black Cat Café. He sometimes went to The Thalia Music Hall, where six hundred dance girls, ladies with winsome smiles and easy grace, were employed. Ed Graney's poolroom was the hangout for Jim Jeffries, Bob Fitzsimmons, and Abe Attel— all great fighters. Negros and O'Brien's was a favorite spot, especially for newspapermen before payday. For seventy-five cents, a customer was served an eight-course dinner, with wine, and could listen to the music and dance all night. A stout, friendly youngster named Paul Whiteman played the violin at Negros and O'Brien's.

The rich man who inhabited the night spots and wore the proper adornments was called a "hot sport." A man who wished to win this classification must have his person well decorated with diamonds and gold. Al did his best to become a hot sport, but though he did manage to embellish his vest with a few gold accoutrements, he was never able to reach the diamond class. He could only admire the diamond studs, and envy the gold claw ring, which was usually set with a large diamond and sparkled like a bright star on the hot sport's middle finger when he embraced a champagne glass.

The thick heavy watches the men carried were called turnips, and almost every male wore a gold watch chain suspended between the lower pockets of his vest. The prosperous sport would hang from his watch chain as many gold implements and other paraphernalia as he could safely carry. Standard equipment included a gold knife, a gold cigar cutter, a gold toothpick, and a gold ear-cleaner. The ear-cleaner, a small spoonlike object, could be used either for digging impediments out of the ears or for cleaning pipes. Runyon used a matchstick to clean his ears. The adornments of a hot sport were more than a symbol of his prosperity. When his gambling fortunes took a bad turn, or a series of café checks overpowered his pocketbook, he could convert his jewelry into cash in any pawnshop. Since a sport carried his capital on his person, where it could be seen, everyone knew he was broke when he appeared in public unadorned. It was then considered proper for all the hapless sport's friends to buy him drinks.

The wealthy and socially prominent of San Francisco were settled at the top of the city on Nob Hill, which over-looked Chinatown and the bordello district. At one time 3800 girls welcomed callers in their "cribs" and in the luxurious parlor houses, where the madams, who were among the most popular and influential women in town, presided with discriminating taste and decorum.

In Chinatown it was not uncommon to see derelicts stretched out on boards in the street smoking opium, which was sold for twenty-five cents a toy of hop. As a reporter, Runyon found all this activity an integral part of life—flagrant, immoral, imperfect, sometimes sordid, but always interesting. He was particularly amused by the attitude of the San Francisco newspaper publishers, who, because they refused to countenance any advertisements that might jeopardize the morals of their readers, frowned on copy that mentioned intimate wearing apparel such as women's stockings.

Al liked San Francisco. But in 1910, when Van Loan asked Runyon to come to New York, Al packed his bags immediately.

5

BY-LINE—DAMON RUNYON

Al made one detour on his way to New York. He stopped
in Denver long enough to marry Ellen Egan, daughter of
the editor of the *Denver News*. Ellen was a society reporter
for the *News*. Runyon had met her when he was complet-
ing his newspaper stint in Denver. When New York called
for him, Al decided that he and Ellen would go together,
hand in hand, into the city. The bride and bridegroom
arrived in New York early in 1911 and went to live in a
boarding house in Flushing, Long Island.

When the *New York American* offered Van Loan a position on the newspaper's sports staff, he turned it down, recommending Runyon for the job. Al accepted immediately, and when he learned that his starting salary was to be $40 a week he was flabbergasted. "Why, managing editors don't get that much out where I come from," he remarked.

Runyon's first big assignment was to cover the baseball activities of the New York Giants, who were to train that spring in Dallas, Texas. One day before the training season began he was sitting at his desk in the city room trying to form the lead for one of his stories. The lead would not come. He smoked a cigarette and toyed with the keys of his typewriter. He wrote "By Alfred Damon Runyon" at the top of the page, and lighted another cigarette. He stared at the wall; sometimes a reporter's mind finds it more convenient to write the lead on the wall first. Finally the lead came, and the rest of the story followed easily, paragraph after paragraph.

Al handed the story over to Harry Cashman, the sports editor. Cashman read it, and then took a pencil and scratched off one of the names on the by-line.

"Runyon," Cashman called.

Al hurried to the editor's desk.

"I don't like that by-line," he said dryly. "Three names won't do for a by-line. From now on you're Damon Runyon."

"Damon Runyon? Damon Runyon?" Al said, sounding the name carefully, distinctly.

Cashman looked at Al for the first time, surprised that his decision was being questioned. "Yeah, Damon Runyon," he said, returning to his work.

"Yeah, Damon Runyon," Al repeated, with exaggerated good humor. "It sounds kind of nice, and musical. Well, I guess that's the end of Al Runyon."

It was the end of Al Runyon, the name, all right.

When Damon joined the Giants spring training camp at Dallas, it was the first time he had entered into open, free-style competition with the New York writers. He proceeded cautiously at first, and then decided to abandon conventional reporting. He began filing feature stories, fresh, colorful, humorous, as a substitute for straight, factual sports writing. The flamboyant extroversion of one player, "Bugs" Raymond, supplied Damon with the material for most of his stories. Soon, nearly everyone in New York was familiar with Bugs Raymond, the erratic, daffy pitcher of the New York Giants, and people were buying more and more *Americans* to read about him.

Although they were a bit startled to find a new member of the staff assuming the stature of a star reporter almost overnight, the editors of the *American* were wearing noticeable smiles and congratulating themselves on their astuteness in hiring Runyon. The editors wired Runyon to send more of the same. When the paper needed a straight news story they could use the accounts that came in on the wire services, but not every reporter could write well enough to make readers demand his individual story. Damon knew what he was doing; he was putting his best foot forward and writing the type of story that would make his name known.

Returning from Dallas, Damon stopped off in Arizona at a camp for tubercular people to visit his father. Alfred's battle to regain his health was almost lost now. After his son had left Pueblo, Alfred had moved to Pikes Peak,

Colorado, believing that clear air might relieve his condition. He established a small local paper, *The Pikes Peak Express,* and resumed work with a new vigor and spirit, hoping for the best. But he soon knew that he was too ill to work, and decided to try the camp in Arizona for a while.

"Well, son, your old man is now just a candle of spirit wrapped in flesh and bones, and a thin candle at that," Alfred said, after he greeted Damon. "The other day the prettiest nurse you'd want to place your arms around walked by here, and I was just too tired to get out of my chair and talk to her. . . . It's one thing to be too tired to talk, but when you don't have enough energy to talk to a young lady it means age, and plenty of it."

"Don't let that worry you, old man," Damon replied. "You just haven't thawed out from winter yet."

"Yes, I'll be glad when it's warm again," Alfred said quietly. "Well, now that you've hit the big time, I suppose all the Renoyans and Runyans, and Runyons should be proud. It has been a long way from one Manhattan to the next Manhattan. What's that you're doing, seeing ball games and writing about them? Is that reporting, Al?"

"It's the best kind of reporting, old man," Al replied. "I get paid for enjoying myself."

"Maybe you're right, Al," Alfred said, reflectively. "There's one thing I want to say to you, son. Don't start copying those other big reporters. You write it your own way. Write it so people will want to read your stuff because it's different. A good reporter who can't get any offhand humor or interest in his story is just another reporter."

"I know what you mean, old man," Damon said, with fresh enthusiasm. "You can teach any intelligent kid the mechanics of reporting: how to round up all the facts and assemble them into a story that will satisfy the city desk, and inform the reader. But that's not the art of reporting. When you can put not only facts into your story, but color, feeling, human interest as well, then you're an artist."

Damon smiled warmly at his father. The old man was pleased.

"By the way, old man," Damon whispered, as though conveying a secret. "You can't call me Al any more. My name's Damon Runyon now."

"Damon Runyon, Damon Runyon," Alfred said, skeptically. "You ought to wear a carnation in your lapel with a name like that."

"I think I will," Damon remarked.

A few months after Damon's visit, Alfred realized that he could now surrender peacefully, and with honor. He moved to Clovis, New Mexico, where a number of his cronies from Kansas had settled. A short time later he died. Damon had been shocked at the knowledge that Alfred was dying, beyond all physical help. He was surprised that there was a part of him that wished to turn to prayer. When he realized that his father's death was imminent, Damon expressed his prayer in a poem, "The Song of the Exiles." One verse read:

Our doctor-generals have kept our camps flung wide 'neath the
      Southwest skies;
And we've fought our batteries of great resolve with a courage
      that never dies;

So we spend our time on the sun-splashed plain that the healing
      South Wind sweeps—
And each morning that marshals our thin reserves finds our
      dreams lying dead in heaps!
   So we kneel when darkness comes, and pray—
   (There's very little that we can say;)
   "Lord, Oh, Lord, Give us this day—
      Be with us;
      Stay with us!"

The *American* editors, reasoning that it would be foolish
to restrict Runyon's writing to the sports page, were determined to employ his talents wherever they would do the
most good. While working under the sports editor, Damon
was to travel with the New York ball teams, devoting his
attention to color and personalities, and ignoring the
technical details of the game. But he also received assignments—the best assignments—from the city desk.

Early in 1912, Damon was sent to Mexico to cover the
revolution against the Madero government. This bit of
internecine business was interesting because the revolt
was being conducted against a man who was attempting
to give his country a constitutional government. Damon
took the revolution in his stride, filing competent stories,
but finding the affair only mildly interesting, and not
nearly as exciting as the Spanish-American War.

Runyon returned from Mexico in time to report his first
big murder trial, the celebrated Rosenthal murder case.
The story focussed his attention on the New York underworld, and his interest in this assorted breed of criminals
and racketeers became a lifelong hobby. He was completely fascinated by this home-grown, complicated system

of crime. The purpose of the underworld leaders was to
live in royal, though illegal, style, and to protect their
position by the principles of coercion and intimidation;
failing in this, by bribery and murder. The police had to be
bribed; opponents of the presiding royalty, and informers
within the ranks, had to be murdered.

On July 16, 1912, Herman Rosenthal, a gambling-house
proprietor, was shot and killed while standing outside the
Metropole Hotel, on Forty-third Street, not far from
Times Square. Although seven policemen were near the
scene of the crime at the time, the assassins escaped. It
was soon learned that this was an interlocking case of
bribery and informing. Rosenthal had charged that he and
other gamblers had been forced into partnership with a
New York police lieutenant, and said he was ready to
recite names and details to the district attorney.

Since Rosenthal had announced his intention of turning informer, he had certainly provided a handsome
motive for his murder. District Attorney Charles Whitman
had little trouble adding two and two. Two weeks after
the murder, Police Lieutenant Charles Becker, who had
been able to make bank deposits of $65,000 on a salary of
$2,250 since November 1911, was arrested and indicted
for instigating the crime. The crew of murderers was com-
posed of "Gyp the Blood" Horowitz, "Lefty" Louis Rosen-
berg, "Whitey" Lewis, and "Dago" Frank Ciroficci. "Baldy
Jack" Rose, who was also involved in the crime, turned
state's evidence. Lieutenant Becker and the four murderers
were convicted of first-degree murder, and later died in
the electric chair in Sing Sing.

Damon reported the case, but he was not content merely

to cover the facts as they developed. He began exploring
the underworld, becoming acquainted with its inhabitants
by frequenting their side-street bars and backroom gather-
ing places. He was able to associate with these dark
characters without antagonizing them or arousing their
suspicion. Somehow he convinced them that he was but
a harmless bystander, a sympathetic ear. Yet, through
these associations, but without placing his life or soul in
jeopardy, he later gained a good-sized share of the world's
goods, when he made them into the basic ingredients for
his short stories. And when he became the benevolent
chronicler of the New York tribe of the unlawful, its
citizens boasted of their friendship with Runyon.

Damon was still a fledgling baseball reporter when he
first met Irvin S. Cobb in the press box at the Polo Grounds.
Cobb was then a famous rewrite man on Charley Chapin's
Evening World. Bozeman Bulger, the baseball writer for
the *World,* had appointed himself Damon's guardian in
these early days, and it was through Bulger that Damon's
close friendship with Cobb developed. Damon considered
Cobb the greatest newspaperman in town and, when it
was reported that Cobb's salary was $90 a week, Damon
said this was a fantastic wage, but pointed out that it only
justified his ranking Irvin as the incomparable reporter of
his time. Cobb had sold a short story to George Horace
Lorimer of the *Saturday Evening Post,* and it was universally agreed that he was only one step from the newspaper rewrite desk to the world of literature. But Cobb
was not willing as yet to forsake his regular job for the
bright promise of a literary future. He spent his days off
in the press box, telling stories in a soft southern accent,

and allowing his strong, bellowing laugh to echo over the Polo Grounds, spreading consternation among the players and confusion in the stands.

Runyon and Cobb were among the members of the baseball clique who bought an old pot-bellied boat, which they harbored at Seaford, on Long Island, voyaging into the Sound during every season and in all weather. They sailed out to fish in the summer, to shoot shore birds in the fall, and ducks and geese in the winter. Sometimes unexpected freezing temperatures settled over the water, stilling its motion in ice, and isolating the sportsmen for several days. But when Cobb was along what would have been a desperate situation turned into a delight. Damon said they would eat, drink, and sleep, and listen to the warmth of Cobb's voice telling stories. His fund of tales seemed to be endless, a continuity of entertainment, always flowing with imagination and tasteful variety from some infinite source. Cobb was never known to be unavailable for a hunting trip, and the group used to go as far as Nova Scotia after moose. Neither Damon nor Cobb cared particularly for fishing or shooting birds, but the trips gave them the occasion for practicing their real hobbies—eating, drinking, and talking. It was obvious that Damon bowed to Cobb as the great man, and he proved this by never attempting to hold the center of the stage when Irvin was in his company. Damon loved to eat, but he admitted that Cobb was his superior in this field of endeavor, too.

"He was at his best in boots and canvas clothing before a roaring fire in the woods surrounded by hairy-chested guys who could eat and drink in quantity," Damon once remarked. "I think in those days Cobb was the greatest singlehanded trencherman alive."

Franklin P. Adams, a man of considerable erudition, who was writing a newspaper column at the time, sat in the press boxes occasionally, although the baseball writers never welcomed him with the same fondness they showed for Cobb. F. P. A. had assigned himself the post of watchdog of the English language and took delight in calling public attention to the grammatical misdemeanors of newspaper reporters. When F. P. A. pointed in print to a slip of Damon's, he passed a sleepless night worrying over the criticism, and then determined that the matter could best be resolved by his directing one well-aimed fist at the columnist's nose, but he was restrained from taking this course of vengeance by wiser men. Damon said that his error in grammar was caused by pure ignorance and thought Adams had taken unfair advantage of him. Meanwhile, F. P. A. would stroll blithely into the press boxes and sit among the men who were the victims of his most caustic barbs. Adams' remarkable aplomb in the presence of the baseball writers struck Damon as being odd, and he once remarked, "I often thought that if he could have read their minds he would have chosen a seat in the right field bleachers."

Newspapermen at that time believed that a number of young writers were fired because of the publicity F. P. A. gave to their mistakes in grammar, but Damon said he doubted this popular rumor, although he did know that Adams often came close to breaking a young writer's heart by nailing him to a grammatical cross. Runyon never forgot the attention F. P. A. gave his grammar, and many years later, when his own writing ability was secure and beyond the reach of grammar critics, he remembered the incident with some bitterness.

"Some of the boys thought Adams had a mean streak in him," Runyon wrote. "I never believed that. It was my opinion that while he was often unkind, he was unwittingly so, and that it was due more to lack of human warmth and sympathy in his make-up than anything else. In other words, I do not think Adams would have deliberately hurt anyone's feelings, and I think he was generally surprised when he did. It is possible, too, that he was motivated by a genuine desire to improve the grammar of the baseball writers and thought that criticism was the best means of achieving the purpose. If that was his idea, I fear he did not meet with much success. Baseball writing continued grammatically good, bad and indifferent during his time, just as it was before and just as it is today. It distresses me to report that Adams had no effect one way or the other. I do not need him now to tell me that the way I have been saying things all my life is dead wrong, though he can no longer hurt my feelings by mentioning it."

When he had the money, Damon liked to eat in Broadway's best restaurants and to drink in quantity, a habit that quickly dissipated the strength of his wallet. Near the end of the week he was forced to budget himself to thirty cents a day, but he had evolved a routine for seeing him through his days of impoverishment. He went to Coddington's for breakfast, where he'd order a five-cent glass of beer, and took his first nourishment for the day from the free lunch counter. Lunchtime would find him at Dowling's, with two five-cent glasses of beer and a snack from the free lunch counter. In the afternoon he usually dropped into Frank Geraghty's for a beer and a taste of the salami. Dinner was usually at Mack's—two glasses of beer, and several liberal helpings of pickles, a plate of herring, and hard-boiled eggs. Despite the limitations of his salary, Damon knew what level he wanted to live on, and he refused to compromise, nor would he forego the luxuries he couldn't afford.

Damon always had trouble with his feet. He blamed this unhappy condition on two unnatural forces in his past life: first, the long boyhood years he trod the streets of Pueblo in his bare feet, and second, the number of miles he was forced to tramp carrying a full pack during his soldiering days. He developed a complex about the pain and discomfort his feet caused him, and whenever he reached a temporary state of affluence his first act was to spend fifty dollars for a pair of shoes. His interest in everything that concerned a pair of shoes was almost an obsession. One day, during his early life in New York, he was strolling along Fifth Avenue when an object in a luggage store caught his eye. He stopped and stared into the window, transfixed for several minutes. It was a shoe trunk.

"To show you how a little thing can influence a man, I will tell you about the shoe trunk I bought when I first came to New York City," Damon said, recalling the incident later.

"It was a beautifully made thing of some durable wood covered with shining yellow sole leather with lock and hasps of brass the rich color of newly minted gold, a work of art if ever there was one.

"It was lined with soft material like canton flannel and

it had compartments for about eight pairs of shoes, each of which could be wrapped in pieces of that same flannel-like material before being stowed away in a compartment. There was a tray that lifted out and under the tray was space for a pair of riding boots.

"The whole trunk was amazingly neat and compact and could easily be carried by the leather handle on top or one of the leather handles on either end. . . .

"The price was $65 which is not much more than the price of a shoe shine nowadays but was then a neat sum of money. I venture the opinion that if the same trunk were manufactured now you could not buy it under two hundred dollars. And $65 was the exact amount I received one day from Bob Davis, then editor of *Munsey's,* for a short story and it was the most money I had had in my pocket in a long time.

"Now I had never seen a shoe trunk before in my life. I had never even heard of one. I had one $3 pair of shoes, which was all I ever owned at one time and I was fresh in from Colorado where one pair of shoes at a clip was deemed ample by most of our citizens, though there were rumors of some with several pairs.

"My purchase of the thing puzzles me to this day.

"I have a vague feeling that the salesman may have been a trifle superior . . . as he informed me of the uses of the trunk and that my purchase was in a spirit of defiance of the big town generally—a gesture to show it that I was no neckyoke even if I was a new arrival and that I was not to be intimidated by a shoe trunk. Or maybe I wanted to impress that salesman with the idea that I had been accustomed to buying shoe trunks all my life.

"Anyway I plunked down the $65 and told him to stencil

my initials in either end and deliver it to a home in Flat-bush where I was staying at the time, and incidentally was in the red for board and room deeper than even friendship justified. I shall never forget the expressions of amazement on the faces of my hosts when the shoe trunk arrived the next day, packaged like some great treasure six layers of wrapping paper thick, and were told what it was.

"They never said anything in criticism to me about it then or afterwards, though it seems to me that the sheer idiocy of the purchase of an expensive shoe trunk by an impecunious young man with practically his last dollar must have called for some discussion in private. I know I asked myself many a time, Runyon, why the heck did you buy that trunk? I never found a satisfactory answer.

"But it served two purposes. It inspired me to greater industry than was my habit to get money to buy enough shoes to fill the trunk and, in the process of acquisition, I paid my board bill."

In 1913, the New York Giants and the Chicago White Sox made a round-the-world tour playing exhibition ball games. Damon's first assignment of the year was to pick them up when they reached England. The reception he received in London astonished him. The English news-papermen feted him in the royal style usually reserved for a conquering hero. He was wined and dined and in-troduced to important dignitaries. Damon knew of no precedent for his welcome; in America a newspaperman was accepted as one of the commonest of workmen, like the motorman on the Third Avenue trolley. He asked his hosts if they hadn't mistaken him for Teddy Roosevelt. They assured him that they knew his identity; he was

Damon Runyon, a romantic figure out of the Wild West, and a great newspaperman. When Damon returned to New York he was not a little spoiled by his London success. He later admitted that he now had "all the privileges, if not the temperament, of a trained seal and the cubs regarded me with awe."

One day late in 1913 Damon awoke on a train speeding west five hundred miles out of New York City. His face had been pressed against the windowpane and the late afternoon sun had been shining on him for hours. His head hurt, his mouth was sticky and dry as though he had been eating cheese, his stomach was sick, and his face was dirty. He recognized the familiar signs of cause and effect. He had been drinking and now he must suffer. That was simple enough. But what was he doing on this train? He stood up and looked through the car, expecting to find a group of friendly faces—his fellow baseball writers. They must all be journeying to an assignment; he had got drunk, and they had loaded him onto the train. Perhaps they were headed for the World Series. That was logical.

Damon asked the conductor which direction they were headed. West! No, that wasn't correct. Philadelphia had won the American League pennant, and the New York Giants held the National League flag. He reflected on this a moment. "My God, this is terrible. I've lost my mind. Philadelphia has already won the series." Damon looked at the other faces in the car; they stared back, some with pity, others with disdain. "How long have I been drunk?" he wondered. "One, two, three days, a week?" He couldn't remember. "If whiskey can do this to me, John Barleycorn and I had better part company," he muttered, with a fine show of determination. "I've gone on the wagon before, but this time I mean it. A guy who drinks like I do hasn't got a chance."

When Damon returned to New York he insisted that he had permanently severed his friendship with all forms of alcohol. But a man's desire for liquor cannot easily be returned to a dormant stage after enjoying unfettered freedom for a number of years. It was a struggle. Every time Damon felt an unbearable urge for a drink of whiskey, he ordered a cup of coffee. By the time he had conquered his desire for liquor, he was an habitual coffee drinker. He began drinking twenty to forty cups a day. During this transitional period, his disposition soured, and his temper reached an extremely low boiling point. One morning Jerome Beatty, who was then a newcomer to the writing profession, asked Damon a simple question. Damon was just sipping his first cup of coffee for the day, and under these conditions the question sounded like an insult, or at least the remark of a fresh guy who was trying to start an argument. "Who the hell asked you for your opinion?" Damon snarled. As soon as he finished his coffee, Damon went looking for Beatty. When he found him, he apologized for his rudeness, and explained that before he had his first cup of coffee his nerves were so raw he was unable to function in a civilized manner.

The day after Christmas in 1908, Jack Johnson, the Negro fighter, defeated Tommy Burns of Canada in a fight at Sydney, Australia, and returned to the United States as the heavyweight champion of the world. There was almost unanimous agreement among fight fans that Johnson was the greatest heavyweight of his time, and it seemed that he would retain his title, turning back all "white hopes" as long as he could stand on his legs. Johnson had several ounces of gold teeth in his mouth, and when he knew his opponent was not dangerous, he would show his famous "golden smile," and exchange quips with the ringside spectators. But when the contender displayed a semblance of power and aggressiveness, the golden smile disappeared, and Johnson became as fierce and deadly as a jungle animal.

It was inevitable that Johnson's continued mastery over white men in the ring would disturb and anger many Americans, but the fighter didn't trouble himself to aid the cause of racial tolerance by his personal conduct. He had been jailed several times on various charges ranging from breaking the peace to bigamy, and had a propensity for marrying white women, one of whom committed suicide.

In 1913 Johnson was arrested for violating the Mann Act. Lucille Cameron, a nineteen-year-old white girl from Minnesota, was to be the principal witness against him, but Johnson married her before the trial. There were other witnesses, however, and the champion was convicted and sentenced to a year and a day in jail. The case was appealed, but before any action was taken, Johnson slipped out of Chicago disguised as one of Foster's Giants, a Negro baseball team, and took refuge in Europe. He soon became lonesome for the South Side of Chicago, however, and moved to Mexico, perhaps hoping that in some manner he could return to the United States. He became a professional bullfighter for a time to keep himself in money. Then, in 1915, came the offer to fight Jess Willard in Havana. Johnson agreed to the terms, which included a $30,000 guarantee for the match.

This was big news in the sporting world, and Runyon, who had become an inveterate boxing fan, was delighted with his assignment to cover the fight. Damon said that his story on this bout was the best individual piece of sports writing of his career.

The result of the match started a controversy that has never been settled. In the twenty-sixth round Johnson fell to the floor of the ring, and raised his hand to his eyes as if to shield them from the sun. Jess Willard, the huge former cowpuncher from Kansas, was the new champion of the world. Everyone liked the good-natured, amiable Willard, but no one considered him a great fighter. It was incredible that he could knock out Johnson. The cry of "fix" echoed from the ringside in Havana to the small barrooms throughout the United States. Invariably the main theme of all these discussions was contained in a single sentence, "Didn't Johnson use his glove to protect his eyes from the sun while he was being counted out?" The implications of this indisputable fact were intended to end all controversy about whether or not Johnson actually threw the fight.

The fighter himself only added to the confusion of the argument by confessing at one time that he had thrown the fight and then denying it at another. But Runyon, who was not only an accurate reporter, but always seemed to possess information on what was happening behind the scenes, denied that Johnson had deliberately lost the fight. He said the Negro champion wasn't physically able to stand up to another round.

Three decades later the controversy was still going strong. Runyon felt compelled to write a final account of the fight. This is his story:

"To the house in Havana where black Jack Johnson, heavyweight champion of the world, was living on April 5, 1915, went Jack Curley, promoter of the title fight impending for that afternoon between Johnson and Jess Willard, the Kansas giant.

"'Here's the rest of your money, Champ,' said Curley, tossing a bundle of currency on a table. There was $29,000 in the wad, Johnson's guarantee for the fight, less $1,000 he had drawn in advance to buy his white wife, Lucille Cameron, a ring.

"'Put it away, mamma,' said Johnson, handing the money to her, 'and let's get ready to go to the arena.'

"'You aren't thinking of going to the fight, are you, Lucille?' asked Curley. 'You know there'll be very few women there and something might happen to cause you embarrassment. You shouldn't go.'

"The woman, tucking the money into the bosom of her dress, started to cry. Big Johnson stared at Curley, reached over and patted her hand soothingly and said:

"'Aw, Jack's just kidding you, mamma. Of course, you're going.'

"She went. She occupied a front box at the ringside at Marinao race track that hellish hot day watching her huge ebon husband shuffling about the canvas with the white contender. At the close of the twentieth round, Johnson beckoned Harry Frazee, theatrical man and one of Curley's backers, to the ringside and asked him to find Curley.

"It was not until a couple of rounds more had passed that Frazee located the promoter and Johnson asked Curley to take Mrs. Johnson from the arena. In the twenty-fifth round the white woman was being escorted from her box when Willard knocked Johnson down in a corner in front of her and she let out a scream that was heard all over the crowd.

"In the twenty-sixth, Johnson took the full count shielding his eyes from the sun with his gloved hands and for 29 years he has pointed to this fact as implying he knew what he was doing all the time, which no one who saw the fight ever doubted. He simply couldn't go farther. But instead of making capital of his exploit in standing up 26 rounds at the age of 37 to the young giant, Johnson has always seemed to try to cast a shadow on Willard's victory.

"My friend Paul Gallico, a swell mugg but as naive and trusting as all git out, had a yarn in a magazine as a quote from Johnson per Jimmy Johnston (no relation) that the reason he stuck it out for 26 rounds was because the guarantee was belatedly paid Mrs. Johnson at the ringside and that she waved her husband to do his fadeout. To which I say nuts. I have told you when and how the money was paid.

"The excuse Johnson is alleged to have given Johnston for chucking the title is his mother was ill and some mysterious 'boys' had promised to have a deportation ban on him lifted so he could return to the United States and visit his stricken parent but that 'the boys' double-crossed him on that promise. I say nuts to that too, because the case was in the hands of the feds who were not making deals with the likes of Johnson.

"Well, about 95 per cent of all sports tradition is pure fiction. Lies if you like. But harmless. Who the hell cares if long after a sports event the facts get a little twisted."

On March 16, 1916, General Francisco "Pancho" Villa, the most colorful of the Mexican revolutionists, angry because the United States had recognized a Mexican government opposed to him, led four hundred of his soldiers across the border in an attack on Columbus, New Mexico. He partly burned the town and killed nine civilians and eight American soldiers from a nearby army camp. President Wilson ordered Brigadier General John J. Pershing to lead a military expedition of 6000 men into Mexico to capture Villa and bring him back to the United States for trial. Runyon was named one of the four accredited correspondents who were to accompany General Pershing in his search for Villa. It was while covering this punitive expedition into Mexico that Damon's stories appeared for the first time as a syndicated feature in the Hearst press.

After the Columbus raid, Pancho and his band disappeared into the mountains. If Pershing had been equipped with airplanes, he might have been able to spot Villa's hideout, but under the circumstances it was an impossible chase. But the Americans did manage to find a battle. It had been expected that the Mexican government would help the Americans in their hunt for Villa. Instead, General Jacinto Irevino, the Mexican commander in the north, demanded that Pershing leave Mexican soil and warned him that any deviating of his troops would be resisted with force. On June 21, a segment of the American troops clashed with the Mexicans near Carrizal.

In the *New York American* on July 6, 1916, instead of Runyon's usual news story, two of his ballads appeared side by side. One of them concerned the recent battle of Carrizal, and the other went back to a similar American

punitive expedition at Vera Cruz in 1914. At that time
President Wilson ordered American marines and sailors to
take Vera Cruz, when the Mexican government refused to
render special honors to the American flag in atonement
for the temporary arrest of American sailors by the Mexican
army. Damon's ideas on the futility of war had not changed
since he wrote a poem on the charge at Marishoa during
the Philippine Insurrection. His writing was never deeply
philosophical, and he rarely attempted to touch the serious
notes of life. But when he saw men losing grasp of the
basic, rational concepts of civilization, he became angry
with their stupidity. What he had to say was simple and
unhampered by literary or metaphysical trappings. Anyone could understand his theme. "What's the good of it
all?" he inquired

VERA CRUZ
1914

Ho, we went to Vera Cruz
To the doby walls of Vera Cruz;
Ships and men to Vera Cruz—
    Hark to Glory's call!

Rattle o' guns at Vera Cruz,
Ho, the flag swung high at Vera Cruz,
Ho, hearts beat high at Vera Cruz
    As we marched to Glory's call!

Ho, we came from Vera Cruz,
From the fever swamps of Vera Cruz—
What did we do at Vera Cruz
    When we marched to Glory's call?

What did we do at Vera Cruz?
Ho, the buzzard that sweeps o'er Vera Cruz
Knows what we did at Vera Cruz—
    Hark to Glory's call!

Ours are dead at Vera Cruz—
What was the good of it all?

CARRIZAL
1916

Ho, we rode to Carrizal
To the sandy hell of Carrizal
Boot-to-boot to Carrizal—
    Hark to the bugle call!

Swish of bullets at Carrizal
Back-to-back at Carrizal—
Twenty to one at Carrizal—
    Hark to Glory's call!

Ho, we came from Carrizal
From the pit of Hell at Carrizal—
And what did we do at Carrizal
    When we rode to Glory's call?

What did we do at Carrizal?
Ho, the carrion crew at Carrizal
Knows what we did at Carrizal—
    Hark to Glory's call!

Ours are dead at Carrizal—
What was the good of it all?

For a time it appeared as though the United States had

maneuvered itself into a formal, all-out war with Mexico.
The Mexicans, however, sent a conciliatory note to President Wilson promising to do everything in their power to
prevent future outrages against the United States. On
January 28, 1917, the War Department announced that
Pershing had been ordered to withdraw from Mexico. A
note could have been appended to the Army's statement,
pointing out that the United States was about to test its
power in a war of such vast proportions as to make trifling
in Mexican revolutions rather embarrassing.

On April 5, Congress passed a joint resolution authorizing
and directing the President "to carry on war against the
Imperial German Government and to bring the conflict
to a successful termination." The next day President
Wilson issued a proclamation declaring war on Ger-
many.

Damon became a war correspondent. He was assigned
to Camp Upton, and then shuttled between Camp Upton,
Camp Mills, Camp Dix, and Camp Meade. He soon found
that his sympathy for army methods had not warmed one
single degree in eighteen years. He voiced the universal
cry of all soldiers in a poem called "The First Night at
Yaphank."

> I'm there with two thin blankets,
>   As thin as a slice of ham.
> A German spy was likely the guy
>   Who made 'em for Uncle Sam.
> How did I sleep? Don't kid me!
>   My bedtick is filled with straw,
> And lumps and humps, and big fat bumps
>   That punched me 'til I'm all raw.

> Me, and my two thin blankets,
>   As thin as the last thin dime—
> As thin, I guess, as a chorus girl's dress—
>   Well, I had one hell of a time!
> I'd pull 'em up from the bottom—
>   (My nightie's my B.V.D.'s)
> A couple o' yanks to cover my shanks,
>   And then my dogs'd freeze!
>
> You could use 'em for porous plasters,
>   Or maybe to strain the soup.
> (My pillow's my shoes when I try to snooze—
>   And I've chilblains, cough, and the croup.)
> Me, and my two thin blankets,
>   Bundled up under my chin—
> Yes, a German spy was likely the guy,
>   And gosh, but he made 'em thin!

Out at Camp Upton a sergeant named Irving Berlin won the acclaim of all infantrymen when he wrote, "Oh! How I hate to get up in the morning." Damon and other correspondents were filing stories on the completion of a row of barracks or a sewer trench at camp . . . the life-sentence of a deserter . . . 2000 soldiers want to join a correspondence club and write to girls . . . concentrating on French to get ready for Paree . . . small khaki-bound Bibles distributed to all men . . . many a stalwart learning to take out "his housewife kit" and mend socks . . . on Thanksgiving Day every man gets a pound of turkey and a pound of cranberry sauce . . . so keen is the feeling against waste that a major, on seeing a soldier throw away a half-smoked cigarette, teaches him to appreciate its

value by ordering him to bury it in a hole ten feet deep.
One newspaper, apparently convinced that despite the
risks war was fun, carried the comforting headline that
only eleven out of every thousand men are killed in action.
Every soldier could recite the syllogism, "Don't Worry,
Boys," and every vaudeville artist included it as a part of
his repertoire for camp entertainment.

"If the War doesn't end next month, of two things one
is certain: Either you will be sent across the big pond or
you will stay on this side.

"If you stay at home there is no need to worry. If you go
across, of two things one is certain: Either you will be put
on the firing line or kept behind the lines.

"If you are behind the lines there is no need to worry.
If you are at the front, of two things one is certain: Either
you are resting in a safe place or you're exposed to
danger.

"If you are resting in a safe place there is no need to
worry. If you are exposed to danger, of two things one is
certain: Either you're wounded or not wounded.

"If you are not wounded there is no need to worry.
If you are wounded, of two things one is certain: Either
you're wounded seriously or you're wounded slightly.

"If you are wounded slightly there is no need to worry.
If you are wounded seriously, of two things one is certain:
Either you recover or you don't.

"If you recover there is no need to worry. If you don't
recover you can't worry."

Damon went overseas with a contingent from Camp
Upton, and covered the operations of the First Army
during the Argonne and Meuse campaigns. During one

phase of the Argonne drive Runyon was in the front lines
laboring over a story when a shell hit and exploded a short
distance away. Although he and his typewriter were
showered with debris, Damon continued writing, never
taking his eyes off the keyboard. When he finished the
story he looked up inquiringly at the soldiers. They were
staring at him with some suspicion. "Did I hear something?" Damon asked. The soldiers glared at him. A man
with such powers of concentration, they concluded, should
be displayed in a freak show. Damon's favorite offhand
remark of the war was the one Floyd Gibbons attributed
to Sergeant Dan Daly. Daly yelled back at his marines as
he led them out of the trenches in the Boise Belleau.

"Come on you ---- -- ----, do you want to live forever?"

Runyon was with Major General Omar Bundy's Second
Division when they fought at Vaux and were credited with
being responsible for the American successes there. Damon
admired Omar Bundy and his men, especially their ability
to fight.

> Oh, Bundy's Men are big and strong,
>   And gallant, and polite—
> But ask the Bush who fought at Vaux
>   How Bundy's Men can fight!

No special arrangements had been made to ease the
work of the war correspondents. They were neither given
the best billets, nor allotted motor cars for their transportation. Damon didn't particularly care where he slept, but
he was grievously pained by the necessity of covering the
war on foot. He said he hiked "from Etain to the Rhine,"

and declared that it wasn't the screaming shells, the whining bullets, or the unsavory food that caused him to hate war, but his aching feet.

Damon returned to the United States in 1919 aboard the S.S. *Leviathan*. Like the soldiers on board he had tired of the Rhine, of France, of singing "Mademoiselle from Armentières," and was not quite sure now why the war had been fought.

The doughboys returned to a "dry" country, for the Eighteenth Amendment, prohibiting the manufacture, sale, or transportation of liquor, had been passed while they were in Europe. Some people thought this was unfair. The Drys, who had engineered national prohibition into being, believed that the people's appetite for liquor would abate and then stop as soon as there was a law forbidding liquor.

William Jennings Bryan, celebrating his sixtieth birthday at a dry dinner in New York, said, "The liquor issue is as dead as slavery."

Daniel G. Roper, Commissioner of Internal Revenue, declared, "The Prohibition law will be violated—extensively at first, slightly later on; but it will, broadly speaking, be enforced and will result in a nation that knows no alcohol."

When Dr. A. B. Adams, chief chemist of the Treasury Bureau, in charge of testing beverages to guarantee that none surpassed the .5 per cent in alcoholic content permitted by the Volstead Act, was questioned about the possibility of an increase in the home-brewing business, he replied, "Nothing to that. It's too much trouble for uncertain results. They may try it once or twice, but not more." Never before had one country been so plagued with false prophets.

It soon became clear that people who wanted to drink would do so in spite of the law, and would even pay a premium for their desire. In such a situation, there is always someone ready to rake in the profits. This time it was the bootlegger and the speakeasy proprietor—ordinary people, who might never have emerged from the moderate security of the middle classes had not their own lack of scruples helped them to riches. Damon made money on the age of prohibition, too, although he didn't have to break the law to do it, since he was on the wagon. But the new amendment brought into the speakeasies his old friends, the creatures of the underworld. In a speakeasy, everyone was equal, since all were lawbreakers. The ordinary, law-abiding citizens sat at tables adjoining the chronic criminals. While formerly a natural barrier of society, respected by criminal and upright citizen alike, separated these two groups, the speakeasy provided the common denominator that allowed them to develop informal friendships. Damon was a patron of the speakeasy, drinking only coffee, but observing the Pharisees and scoundrels, separately and together. Many of his later short stories were based on a criminal's playing the knight errant to a worldling in distress. The speakeasy brought the burgher and the scapegrace together, and Damon humanized them. He believed that the moral question of drinking was a personal problem, to be decided by individual conscience. If a man determined that liquor was destroying his life, his happiness, and his bankbook, he could, as Damon did, stop drinking. Damon said he personally conquered drink when he discovered that his desire to quit was greater than his craving for liquor.

The sin against logic committed by prohibition amused Damon. In 1920 he was in San Francisco covering the Democratic National Convention, which nominated James M. Cox for President, and Franklin D. Roosevelt for Vice President. One day during the convention he was strolling along the city's streets, pointing out the sights to his three companions, Arthur "Bugs" Baer, Bill Yeager, a San Francisco sports writer, and "Wild" John O'Reilly. They were all in high spirits. Suddenly, for no apparent reason, O'Reilly stopped a stranger in the street, grabbed the lapels of the man's coat with his left hand, and knocked him unconscious with one blow of his right fist. "You Democratic delegate bum," O'Reilly sneered, as the man fell to the pavement. Damon regarded his new pair of shoes with some concern and moved to the edge of the sidewalk. A second stranger, either in self-protection or intending to rectify the injustices in the world, knocked Yeager to the ground with such force that it was several minutes before Bill could regain his feet. Meanwhile, a baker rushed out of his shop near by and knocked out O'Reilly with one blow of his rolling pin. Damon, watching the fight, wondered how the prohibition backers could explain away such occurrences.

During the '20's Runyon's reporting was receiving wide attention. People read his accounts not because the stories were always important, or exclusive news, but because Damon concentrated on some fragment of human interest that the other reporters neglected, or considered trifling. To Damon it wasn't the obtrusive facts that gave a story its meaning, but the undercurrent of drama, the unfolding of personality. His writing was warm and personal, and never burdened with a heavy accumulation of facts. When they read a Runyon story, readers began to feel that the news was a part of their own experience.

One of Damon's assignments was to cover an international yacht race. The fact that he had only a meager knowledge of yachts and was almost completely ignorant of the intricacies of boat racing didn't seem to concern the sports editor and certainly didn't bother Damon. The reporters followed the yachts in a cutter and, while the others watched, talked, smoked and recited jokes, Damon scribbled continuously in his notebook. When the race was over, Damon's story, bursting with descriptive details the other reporters could never hope to remember, was already fashioned in his notebook. The next day every reader, whether he was a yachting enthusiast or not, could understand and enjoy the spectacle of the race by reading Runyon's story.

If Damon's knowledge of yacht racing was limited, he knew very little more about tennis. But he was assigned to cover a championship match in competition with the reporters who specialized in this sport for rival papers. All during the match Damon carefully jotted down notes on the size and shape of the puffs of chalk dust raised by Big Bill Tilden's smashes as compared to the puffs lifted by his opponent. A tennis coach who read Damon's account of the match the next day said it was the best tennis story he had ever read.

One of the printers on the *New York American*, commenting on the Runyon stories, said, "Damon could write a book about one sunrise if he had to do it."

6

BROADWAY BOSWELL

As long as he lived, Damon avoided the bondage of home life; he ignored its reality and almost succeeded in wishing it away. He admitted few friends into his personal life and sometimes refused to recognize its existence even to himself. The dizzy lunge the New York El train made as it careened around Suicide Curve on the way to the Polo Grounds was to Damon one of the satisfying experiences in life. He preferred it to the intimacies of his home. He found more pleasure in observing the joys and

[122]

hopes, the troubles and tragedies in the daily lives of the inhabitants of Broadway than in watching the growth and life of his children. Like his father, he was not a born parent. His marriage was not a success. When Damon's wife, Ellen Egan Runyon, died in Bronxville, New York, in November 1931, he had been separated from her for several years. They had two children: a son, Damon Runyon, Jr., and a daughter, Mary Elaine.

Damon tried to live as close to Broadway as possible, usually making his residence in a hotel room or apartment near the Big Street. At one time he lived at the Gotham Hotel at Fifty-fifth Street and Fifth Avenue, but he soon accumulated several reasons that argued against any further dwelling on Fifth Avenue. He found that the money he paid for a room at the Gotham was not commensurate with the amount of time he spent in the room. The clientele at the Gotham seemed a bit snobbish to a man with Damon's tastes in companions. Then, too, he considered living as far away from Broadway as Fifth Avenue comparable to having your home in the suburbs. Damon hated the suburbs.

The incident that was the immediate cause of his severing connections with the Gotham occurred early one morning when Damon was making his way home after an all-night chit-chat with the citizens of Broadway. He was walking east on Fifty-fifth Street, when a taxidermist who was stuffing a tarpon in his shop on the third floor of an adjacent building lost his grasp on the fish and it slipped out the window. The tarpon hit Damon squarely on the head and knocked him to the ground. The fish was badly damaged.

Since this was the prohibition era, the ordinary person would have accepted this untoward accident as a link in the natural chain of events that accompanied the drinking of liquor in a speakeasy. But Damon had abandoned drinking long ago. He said this incident was just an example of the misfortunes that could happen to a person who deserted Broadway and ventured into unfriendly territory on the East Side. Damon left the Gotham the next day.

One of Damon's favorite homes was the Forrest Hotel, 224 West Forty-ninth Street. For a time he kept a big white cat and a cricket as pets in his apartment. When the inevitable occurred and the cat ate the cricket, Damon was so upset over the loss of his little friend that he disposed of the cat.

Damon conducted Broadway seminars both in his room and in the lobby of the Forrest Hotel. Although the subjects discussed at these meetings never reached a very high metaphysical plane, there were many scholarly dissertations on the elementary phases of life. Certainly, never before had so many devotees of the pursuit of pleasure gathered together in one place. Regular members at the Forrest forums included Bill Fallon, the attorney; "Butch" Tower, a former actor, now a betting commissioner; Jack Conway, sports writer; Lou Smith, managing director of the Rockingham Race Track; Frank Wrightsman, liquor distiller; and Charles "Chuck" Green. Harry Lenny, Eddie Borden, Eddie Walker, and Joe Jacobs, all fight managers, contributed valuable information and opinions to the sessions.

"Swifty" Morgan, Broadway roustabout, acted as general

factotum for the Broadway coterie, some of whom were Leo Donnelly, the actor; Charley Cooke, the fight manager; Mendel Yudelowitz, the clothing mogul; Joe Benjamin, the fighter; Teddy Hayes, the trainer; Jack Kearns, the enterprising mitt impressario; "Champ" Segal, the pugilist and now manager; and Bozeman Bulger, the writer. David Palter, the "Little Davey" of San Francisco days, was doing very well in Wall Street. He dropped in occasionally at the Forrest to maintain his standing as delegate-at-large. Solly Violinsky, the actor, was gaining his reputation as a Broadway wit.

Across the street from the hotel, Mike Jacobs conducted a theater-ticket office. Damon and Mike became close friends. The late Joe Barberra, who was a Department of Justice agent, used to visit Damon at the Forrest, too. They sometimes passed Christmas together, delivering as many as two hundred turkey baskets to poor families on the West Side.

Almost every night a member of New York's Sanitation Department walked through the lobby of the Forrest and rode an elevator upstairs. Damon was told that the man was visiting a group of bootleggers in the hotel. This practice did not seem to be a part of the business of a street cleaner as outlined in the city charter, so Damon inquired further. Such incongruities piqued his curiosity.

After some intense investigation he learned that the municipal scows engaged in towing refuse out of the harbor were carrying liquor into the city on their return trip. The sanitation men who were in charge of the city's garbage disposal arranged to meet the rum-running fleet outside the harbor and bring the liquor into the city. In this manner an otherwise worthless trip became a profitable enterprise to all concerned and the cargo was protected from the confiscating hands of the harbor police.

The nightly visitor at the Forrest was the liaison agent who arranged the timing of the rendezvous, the transfer of liquor, and other details. Damon considered this one of the more sensible ways for the city to spend the taxpayers' money. It not only supplied the city with a needed commodity but added to the income of some of the lower-paid citizens.

Damon by no means isolated himself at the Forrest. He considered it a duty to tour the night clubs: The Plantation, Connie's Inn, the Helen Morgan Club, and the Club Richman. In the afternoons he visited the race tracks at Jamaica, Belmont, or the Aqueduct, where he was known as an active gambler as well as a working newspaperman.

One of Runyon's occasional stops was the Manister Club, which was operated by "Honest John" Kelly and was the scene of some of the highest stakes in gambling history. On any good night three million dollars would change hands over Honest John's tables. Kelly was at a baseball game the day "One Eye" Connolly, the famous gate crasher, lost his glass eye. Kelly found the glass eye and returned it to Connolly. Because of this singular feat of honesty, Paul Armstrong, the sports writer and playwright, christened Kelly "Honest John."

Whenever Damon went to a New York ball park to cover a baseball game, he usually was greeted by One Eye Connolly, standing in front of the entrance dressed in a green suit. Sewed on the back of his suit coat was the verse:

Of One Eye Connolly
You've often heard tell:
I'll first crash Heaven,
And then crash Hell.

John Coakley and "Baldy" Weiss joined forces with Arnold
Rothstein to succeed Honest John as entrepreneurs of the
dice game, a pastime that in a single night made some
persons wealthy and others paupers. The game was played
every night in a building next door to the Claridge Hotel
on West Forty-fourth Street, off Broadway.

Damon waited in the lobby of the Forrest to welcome
the gamblers when they returned at 5 A.M. "How was it
today?" he would ask. After a short period of commiserat-
ing with the losers (the winners always seemed to disappear before he could congratulate them), Damon would
ask, "What's the line?" His question meant that he wanted
to know the accurate odds on the fights, baseball games,
and all other impending contests. He needed this betting
information for two reasons. First, it was essential for
him to know the odds to carry out his own betting, and
second, as a reporter, Damon believed he was duty bound
to give this news to his readers.

Billy LaHiff's Tavern on Forty-eighth Street became one
of Damon's regular ports of call. Billy had a habit that was
puzzling in a New Yorker. He was helpful to young newspapermen when they most needed a friend.

The rooms over Billy's tavern cradled a nest of fledgling
reporters and columnists, and also harbored a number of
great ambitions, past, present, and future. Walter Winchell
lived there with his bride, June Magee. Walter was ex-

ploring Broadway, seeking a medium where he could best express his talents. "Bugs" Baer and his wife, Jimmy Hussey, the actor, and LaHiff himself occupied apartments in the building. Downstairs in the tavern, the greats of the sports, theater, and newspaper worlds gathered each evening for food and conversation.

One day, Winchell informed LaHiff that he couldn't afford the $150-a-month rental. He was only making $50 a week as a reporter on the *Vaudeville News*.

"Is $125 too much?" asked Billy

"We'll try," replied Walter.

"That's fine," said LaHiff, smiling. "Don't take your baby carriage from the front of the building—it's the only sign of respectability it has!"

Damon later recorded the above in his column.

It was at LaHiff's that Runyon formed the habit of wrapping up tidbits and taking them home with him, apparently storing the food against a possible bad day at the race track. At first he tried to explain away this unconventional habit by telling friends and inquiring waiters that the food was for his favorite cat, or dog, or cricket, or whatever domesticated animal life he happened to be sheltering in his apartment at the time. But he soon stopped apologizing and brazenly pilfered snippets of salami, Nova Scotia salmon, and assorted appetizers without embarrassment.

Eating was one of Damon's great interests in life, and although he usually was within a stone's throw of a restaurant no matter where he went, he liked to carry some food in his pocket in case he wandered too far from the base of supplies.

Damon was one of Arnold Reuben's steady customers when he had his restaurant at Seventy-fourth Street and Broadway. It was Runyon's habit to sit at a side table and chat with Arnold Rothstein, the notorious gambler, or discuss boxing with Jimmy Walker who was then a state senator. One Saturday night Rothstein insisted on occupying a booth all evening much against Reuben's wishes.

"If you hog that booth all night, I lose money," the restaurateur moaned. "Saturday night is one of my big nights."

"I'll pay you for the damn booth," the gambler shouted.

"Okay," Reuben answered. "It's worth $250 to my business tonight."

Rothstein, always a smart money man, jumped from the booth and left the restaurant on the double.

Lindy's restaurant opened in 1921 between Forty-ninth Street and Fiftieth Street. The restaurant eventually became Broadway's town hall, a meeting place where the gentry of the street congregated to eat, discuss business, and loaf. Damon joined the clientele when he discovered the Hungarian goulash, the herring, the cheesecake, the borscht, and the coffee served in Lindy's.

Rothstein made Lindy's one of his unofficial headquarters. On the night of November 4, 1928, while at the restaurant, he received a telephone call. He left immediately to keep an appointment. That night he was found near Broadway with a bullet in his stomach. Later he died of his wound. It was alleged that Rothstein died for failing to make payments on his IOU's.

Because he spent so much time in Lindy's, many people

thought Rothstein owned the restaurant. Even the newspapers reported that Lindy's was the property of the slain gambler. Naturally, Leo Lindeman, the restaurant's real proprietor, was distressed at the printed misstatements and threatened to sue the papers for libel. He asked Damon for advice. For over a week, in every story he wrote on the murder, Runyon printed the names of the actual owners of the restaurant, and offered conclusive proof that Rothstein was in no way affiliated with Lindy's, except as a paying customer. Ironically, the so-called bad publicity the restaurant received as a result of the Rothstein shooting made Lindy's a Broadway institution with a national reputation.

A year later, when George C. McManus, another gambler, went on trial charged with murdering Rothstein, Runyon's knowledge of Broadway gave him an advantage over the other reporters covering the proceedings. Runyon's stories had telling touches of humor and meaning because he knew most of the participants, all citizens of Broadway, better than his first cousins.

One day of the trial he wrote: "Some of the State's witnesses were quite busy at the telephone booths while in the building getting bets down on the Bowie races. It is a severe handicap to summon a man to such a remote quarter as the Criminal Courts Building along toward post time."

The following day Damon reported: ". . . the hours are really tough on a lot of folks who will figure more or less prominently in the trial. Some of the boys were wondering if Judge Nott would entertain a motion to switch his hours around and start in at 4 P.M., the usual hour of adjournment, and run to 10:30 A. M., which is a gentleman's bed-time. The consensus is he wouldn't."

Judge Nott refused to let the state's evidence against McManus go to the jury and directed that a verdict of not guilty be delivered. The murder remained unsolved. But no one was too concerned over this, because Rothstein himself had refused to name his killer before he died although he had ample opportunity. If nothing else, the trial offered clear evidence that there was honor among gamblers on Broadway.

". . . the testimony brought out that 'the master mind,' as the underworld sometimes called Arnold Rothstein, died 'game,' " Damon wrote concerning Rothstein's refusal to talk before he died.

"Game as a pebble.

"In the haunts of that strange pallid man during his life, you could have had 10 to 1, and plenty of it, that he would 'holler copper,' did occasion arise, with his dying gasp.

"Indeed he was often heard to remark in times when he knew that sinister shadows hovered near—and these were not infrequent times in his troubled career, living as he chose to live, 'if anyone gets me, they'll burn for it.'

"And cold, hard men, thinking they read his character, believed they knew his meaning. They felt he was just the kind when cornered by an untoward circumstance, that would squeal like a pig. It shows you how little you really know of a man.

"For when the hour came, as the jury in Judge Nott's court room heard yesterday, with the dismal snow slanting past the windows of the grimy old Criminal Courts

Building—when Arnold Rothstein lay crumpled up with a bullet through his intestines, knowing he was mortally hurt, and officers of the law bent over him and whispered, 'Who did it?' the pale lips tightened, and Rothstein mumbled, 'I won't tell and please don't ask me any more questions.'

"Then another 'sure thing' went wrong on Broadway, where 'sure things' are always going wrong—the 'sure thing' that Rothstein would tell."

Two murder trials, one in 1926, and the other in 1927, were among the biggest news stories of the '20's. The two murders not only contained a full measure of the lurid and morbid details of violent death, but found their motivating force in illicit love. With these ingredients the newspapers were able to supply the public with more than a fair share of vicarious thrills, and almost satiated the readers' appetite for sensation. Damon's stories on these trials gained for him the reputation of being one of the country's greatest reporters.

The Hall-Mills case might have sprung from any community in the country. On September 14, 1922, the Rev. Edward Wheeler Hall, the young rector of the Protestant Episcopal Church of St. John the Evangelist in New Brunswick, N. J., and Mrs. Eleanor Mills, a singer in the church choir, were found slain under a crabapple tree in De Russey's Lane, a well-known trysting place across the Raritan River. The liaison between the Rev. Hall and the leader of his choir had been a topic of gossip among the parishioners and townspeople for a number of years.

The minister had been shot through the head, while Mrs. Mills had been shot three times and her throat was cut so that her head was almost severed, and the windpipe, larynx, and tongue, which the prosecution termed the "singing organs," had been removed. Scattered around the bodies were a collection of love letters the pair had exchanged. The Rev. Hall was married to Mrs. Frances Stevens Hall, a wealthy woman fifteen years older than himself. Mrs. Mills' husband was James Mills, a mild little man who was the janitor in the church.

Four years after the murder, on November 3, 1926, Mrs. Hall and her two brothers, Henry Stevens, a sportsman, who was an expert rifle shot, and Willie Stevens, who liked to wear a fireman's helmet and ride on fire trucks, went on trial for the murder.

". . . the thing has taken on some of the aspects of a big sports event," Runyon wrote on the first day of the trial. "In fact, the telegraph switchboard used for the Dempsey-Tunney fight has been installed in the court house and forty-seven telegraph instruments have been hooked up. An enterprising radio outfit will unofficially broadcast the proceedings, play by play, so to speak. The little town of Somerville, which is the county seat of Somerset County, is all set to take care of a big crowd of visitors, and the indications are that the crowd will be here.

"They would be better off if they remained at home, so far as any chance they have of morbid entertainment is concerned. The court house has a seating capacity of slightly over three hundred, and of this number, one hundred will be representatives of the press and one hundred and eighteen will be witnesses. This will leave room for only about fifty-three casual spectators.

"If speculators could have gotten hold of these extra seats, they would have cleaned up. They could command any price."

The day the husband of the unfaithful choir singer took the stand, Damon wrote:

" 'Jimmy' Mills, husband of the murdered Mrs. Eleanor Mills, and a veritable little mouse of a man, who might have been the cartoonist Opper's original for the harassed Mr. Dubb of his cartoons, was the chief witness for the State today.

"A shoemaker by trade, a church sexton and school janitor by occupation, he is middle-aged and has a peaked face, and sad eyes, and stooped shoulders. His voice is low—an apologetic voice. His manner is self-effacing.

"He is such a man as you might imagine to be a henpecked husband at home, a man bullied by his children and by all the world, a man anybody could push out of their way without protest from him, a harmless, dull little fellow."

The high point of the trial came on November 18, when Jane Gibson, who was known as the "Pig Woman," was carried into the Somerset courthouse and, despite the protests of doctors, testified for four hours as a prosecution witness. She was suffering from cancer.

" 'The Pig Woman' told her story yesterday—told it while stretched out, corpse-like and waxy, on an iron bed in front of the staring jury with a nervous doctor and nurse at her side, and a hospital odor filling the air of the jammed court room," Damon's story began.

"It was an unreal creepy sort of business. Perhaps you can imagine attending a wake, and having the dead sud-

denly begin talking in an out-of-the-grave sort of voice.
This is the way the sick 'pig woman,' officially Mrs. Jane
Gibson, or Easton, talked."

The Pig Woman said she had witnessed the murder of
the minister and his sweetheart, and placed the three defendants under the crabapple tree at the time the crime
was being committed.

" 'The Pig Woman' had been robbed of some corn, and
she had tied her dog to a tree outside the house and she
was sitting listening for marauders. She heard the dog
bark, then she heard a rickety old wagon," Damon's story
continued.

" 'It rattled, and rattled and rattled,' she murmured.

"She went toward her corn field, and she saddled up
Jenny, her mule, and started out on the road to follow the
wagon. She passed an automobile in De Russey's Lane in
which she saw Mrs. Hall and the man she thought was a
colored man.

"Jenny, the mule, brayed, and fearing it would give warning to the corn thieves, she tied the mule to a tree and
proceeded on foot.

" 'I heard voices, mumbling voices, men's voices and
women's voices. I stood still. The men were talking, and
a woman said very quick, "Explain these letters." The men
were saying "G— d— it," and everything else. (She would
not speak the oaths.) Somebody was hitting, hitting,
hitting. I could hear somebody's wind go out and somebody said, "Ugh."

" 'Then somebody said, "G— d— it, let go." A man hol-
lered. Then somebody threw a flashlight toward where
they were hollering. Yes, and I see something glitter, and

I see a man, and I see another man, like they were wrestling together. The light went out and I heard a shot. Then I heard something fall very heavy, and I run for the mule.

" 'I heard a woman's voice say after the first shot, "Oh Henry," easy, very easy, and the other began to scream, scream, scream so loud, "Oh my, oh, my, oh, my," so terrible loud. That woman was screaming, screaming, screaming, trying to get away or something, screaming, screaming, screaming, and I just about got my foot in the stirrup when "Bang, bang, bang," three quick shots.'

"One of the faces she saw, 'the pig woman' said, was the face of Mrs. Hall as she knelt down, fixing something on the ground. Mrs. Hall wore no hat, she said.

"The nurse and doctor raised 'the pig woman' up in her bed so that she faced Mrs. Hall sitting with her relatives.

" 'Do you mind removing your hat, madam,' asked Senator Simpson.

"With a disdainful gesture, Mrs. Hall lifted her black hat from her head, disclosing a wealth of iron-gray hair very carefully groomed, as if she might have been expecting such a request. Mrs. Hall's eyes did not meet the eyes of the staring 'pig woman.'

" 'Is that the woman?' asked Senator Simpson.

" 'Yes,' said 'the pig woman,' and her attendants lowered her down in the bed again."

People considered Willie Stevens the court jester during the trial, but Damon was sympathetic.

"Willie misses very little that goes on in the court, but his interest is that of a child. I am not so sure that Willie comprehends the gravity of this matter. His demeanor in court would indicate no great sense of responsibility.

"You really have to feel sorry for Willie for all he has been depicted as a humorous figure. You would not laugh or joke at him if he were crippled in body, but some people seem to think he is funny because he is somewhat mentally deformed."

On December 3, apparently disbelieving the Pig Woman's story, the jury found the defendants not guilty of the double murder. Mrs. Hall returned to her church work, Henry cleaned his shotgun and went into the woods to hunt, and Willie joined the boys at the fire house to wait for the next alarm.

The next story came a few months later. On March 20, 1927, Albert Snyder, art editor of the magazine *Motor Boating*, was found dead from the effects of chloroform and several blows on his head at his home at 222nd Street, Queens Village, Queens. Police found the house in considerable disorder, with clothes strewn about, and bureau drawers pulled out and emptied. The slain man's wife, Mrs. Ruth Snyder, said burglars had entered the house about 3 A.M., and had knocked her unconscious. When she regained her senses at 7 A.M., she summoned her nine-year-old daughter, Lorraine, and then called the police. For a person who had been unconscious for four hours, Mrs. Snyder seemed remarkably healthy to the police investigating the murder.

The next day Mrs. Snyder confessed that she and Henry Judd Gray, a married salesman of East Orange, N. J., had committed the murder. She said that she and Gray had decided to kill Mr. Snyder because he was becoming suspicious of their illicit love affair. She also claimed that Gray had instigated the murder. Gray was arrested in a Syracuse hotel where he registered the day before the murder to establish an alibi. Gray also confessed. He said he had been coerced into the murder by Mrs. Snyder, who threatened to disclose the details of their affair to Gray's wife.

On the first day of the trial, which began in Long Island City on April 19, Runyon wrote:

"A chilly looking blonde with frosty eyes and one of those marble, you-bet-you-will chins, and an inert, scare-drunk fellow that you couldn't miss among any hundred men as a dead set-up for a blonde, or the shell game, or maybe a gold brick.

"Mrs. Ruth Snyder and Henry Judd Gray are on trial in the huge weatherbeaten old court house of Queens County in Long Island City, just across the river from the roar of New York, for what might be called for want of a better name, The Dumbbell Murder. It was so dumb.

"They are charged with the slaughter four weeks ago of Albert Snyder, art editor of the magazine, *Motor Boating,* the blonde's husband and father of her nine-year-old daughter, under circumstances that for sheer stupidity and brutality have seldom been equalled in the history of crime.

"It was stupid beyond imagination, and so brutal that the thought of it probably makes many a peaceful, home-loving Long Islander of the Albert Snyder type shiver in his pajamas as he prepares for bed.

"They killed Snyder as he slumbered, so they both admitted in confessions—Mrs. Snyder has since repudiated hers—first whacking him on the head with a sash weight, then giving him a few whiffs of chloroform, and finally tightened a strand of picture wire around his throat so he wouldn't revive.

"This matter disposed of, they went into an adjoining room and had a few drinks of whiskey used by some Long Islanders, which is very bad, and talked things over. They thought they had committed 'the perfect crime,' whatever that may be. It was probably the most imperfect crime on record. It was cruel, atrocious and unspeakably dumb."

Later, in describing Mrs. Snyder, Damon reported:

"Her eyes are blue-green, and as chilly looking as an ice cream cone. If all that Henry Judd Gray says of her actions the night of the murder is true, her veins carry ice water. Gray says he dropped the sash weight after slugging the sleeping Snyder with it once and that Mrs. Snyder picked it up and finished the job."

On April 28, Gray's confession was read. Damon had a field day.

"Right back to old Father Adam, the original, and perhaps the loudest 'squawker' among mankind against women, went Henry Judd Gray in telling how and why he lent his hand to the butchery of Albert Snyder.

"She-she-she-she-she-she-she-she. That was the burden of the bloody song of the little corset salesman as read out in the packed court room in Long Island City yesterday.

"She-she-she-she-she-she. 'Twas an echo from across the ages and an old familiar echo, at that. It was the same old 'squawk' of Brother Man whenever and wherever he is in a jam, that was first framed in the words:

" 'She gave me of the tree, and I did eat.'

"It has been put in various forms since then, as Henry Judd Gray, for one notable instance close at hand, put it in the form of eleven long typewritten pages that were read yesterday, but in any form and in any language it remains a 'squawk.'

" 'She played me pretty hard.' . . . 'She said, "You're going to do it, aren't you?" ' . . . 'She kissed me.' . . . She did this. . . . She did that. . . . Always she-she-she-she-she ran the confession of Henry Judd."

Damon's reportorial style was trained to strike each chord of the human emotions at the proper moment. His touch was seldom subtle, but it was always effective. He would scribble out his running story, paragraph by paragraph, and hand it to the telegraph operator, who would relay it to the city desk in time for his deadline. He would write his leads after doing the story itself. Despite the necessity for writing while the events of the courtroom were unfolding before him, in the Snyder-Gray trial, he was able to compose symphonic and integrated stories.

There was tearful sentiment when Mrs. Snyder's daughter was brought into the courtroom to testify.

"Out of the dark tangles of this bloody morass there stepped for a brief moment a wraith-like little figure all in black—Lorraine Snyder, the nine-year-old daughter of the blond woman and the dead art editor. She was, please God, such a fleeting little shadow that one had scarcely stopped gulping over her appearance before she was gone.

"She was asked just three questions by Hazleton as she sat in the big witness chair, a wide-brimmed black hat shading her tiny face, her presence there, it seemed to me, a reproach to civilization.

"Justice Scudder called the little girl to his side, and she stood looking bravely into his eyes, the saddest, the most tragic little figure, my friends, ever viewed by gods or men.

" 'You understand, don't you, that you have to tell the truth?' asked Justice Scudder kindly. I thought he was going to seize the child in his arms.

" 'Yes,' she said faintly.

" 'Then sit right down there and listen carefully,' said Justice Scudder. 'If you do not understand the question just say, "I do not understand." Lean back in the chair and be comfortable. The Court rules the child shall not be sworn.'

"So she sat down and the jurors gazed at her and everybody in the room felt like bawling. Mrs. Snyder gasped and shed tears when her child appeared—tears that probably came from her heart.

"She hasn't seen Lorraine since her arrest. I doubt if Lorraine saw her mother across the big room or that the child fully comprehended where she was. Surely she could not know that all these strange-looking men gathered there were trying to kill her mother. It was a relief when Lorraine left the stand. Two minutes more and they would have been short one reporter in the press section.

" 'Lorraine,' said Hazelton, 'do you remember the morning your mother called you?'

" 'Yes, sir.'

" 'Was it daylight or dark?'

" 'Light.'

" 'And how long after she called you did you call the Mulhausers?'

" 'Right away,' piped the child.

" 'That's all,' said Hazelton.

" 'Not one question by the district attorney, Your Honor,' said Newcombe.

" 'No questions,' said Miller of Gray's counsel.

"Thereafter while Gray was being examined, Mrs. Snyder sat with her elbows on the table, her head bowed, a picture of dejection as great as that presented by Gray for some days. The child seemed to have touched her heart, and the defiant pride with which she has faced her accusers disappeared."

There was a grim sort of comedy when Gray told how he had hit Mr. Snyder over the head with a sash weight.

"Henry Judd has a sash-weight stance much like the batting form of Waner, of the Pittsburgh Pirates. He first removed his big horn-rimmed glasses at Wallace's request.

" 'Show us how you struck.'

" 'I used both hands, like this.'

"So explained the corset salesman, lifting the sash weight, which weighs five pounds, and looks like an old-fashioned coupling pin over his right shoulder. He 'cocked it,' as the ball players would say, pretty well back of his right ear. He is a right-hand hitter."

On May 8, the jury returned a verdict finding both Mrs. Snyder and Gray guilty of murder in the first degree. They were executed in the electric chair at Sing Sing shortly after 11 P.M. on January 13, 1928.

Runyon's reporting technique was designed not merely to relay facts, but to bring his readers as close to the scene of action as was possible through the printed word. Sometimes, as when he covered the trial of Richard Hauptmann for the kidnap-murder of the Lindbergh baby, he used the present tense in the hope that the reader would see and

feel the drama as though he were actually in the courtroom at Flemington, N. J.

"Bruno Hauptmann's supposedly iron nerves fly all to
pieces in a wild outburst in court this afternoon. He suddenly stretches out both arms and yells at Thomas H. Sick,
a young Department of Justice special agent, testifying
on the witness stand:

" 'Mister, mister, you stop lying. You are tellin' a story!'

"His voice, usually described as guttural but now high
and shrill, startles the packed courtroom into one upward
surge, then freezes into a strange silence."

Damon was in Louisville, Kentucky, on May 17, 1940,
when Earle Sande, the jockey, brought in Gallant Fox to
win the Kentucky Derby. In the press box there was the
usual excitement when the horse raced across the finish
line. Then the reporters settled back in their seats, attempting to compose themselves, struggling for the leads
of their stories. Damon showed no emotion. He stood near
his typewriter, lighted a cigarette, and remembered. Sande
had been his favorite jockey since 1922 when he first saw
him bring in a winner for Harry Sinclair. He was then
wearing the white silks of the Rancocas Stable. In 1924,
when Sande was badly hurt in a spill at Saratoga and announced he would never ride again, Damon regarded it
as one of the sporting tragedies of the year. He wrote a
poem that began:

> Maybe there'll be another,
>   Heady an' game, an' true—
> Maybe they'll find his brother
>   At drivin' them horses through.

Maybe—but, say, I doubt it.
　　Never his like again—
　Never a handy
　Guy like Sande
　　Bootin' them babies in!

And now, sixteen years later, Damon was watching him win again. He sat down, placed his cigarette on a table near his typewriter, and began writing. Most of the other reporters have forgotten the stories they wrote that day, but they still remember Damon's lead. It is probably the most famous piece of verse he ever wrote.

Say, have they turned the pages
　Back to the past once more?
Back to the racin' ages
　An' a Derby out of the yore?
Say, don't tell me I'm daffy,
　Ain't that the same ol' grin?
　Why it's that handy
　Guy named Sande,
　Bootin' a winner in!

Say, don't tell me I'm batty!
　Say, don't tell me I'm blind!
Look at that seat so natty!
　Look how he drives from behind!
Gone is the white of the Ranco,
　An' the white band under his chin—
　Still he's that handy
　Guy named Sande,
　Bootin' a winner in!

Maybe he ain't no chicken,
   Maybe he's gettin' along,
But the ol' heart's still a-tickin'
   An' the old bean's goin' strong.
Roll back the years! Yea, roll 'em!
   Say, but I'm young agin,
   Watchin' that handy
   Guy named Sande,
   Bootin' a winner in!

Then Damon began his account of the race.

"Why, it wasn't even close!

"Gallant Fox, pride of the East, with the old master mind of the horsemen sitting in his saddle as easily as if he were in a rocking chair on a shady veranda, galloped off with the $50,000 Kentucky Derby this afternoon. He won by two lengths, going away."

There were two basement cafés on opposite corners of Forty-eighth Street on Broadway during the Golden Age of the '20's. One was the Silver Slipper Café, owned by Billy Duffy and his combination, and the other was the Parody Club, where the entertainment was furnished by Jimmy Durante, Lou Clayton, and Eddie Jackson, one of the most popular teams of café entertainers ever to hit Broadway. The Parody was owned by Big Jim Redmond, and both he and Duffy were golf enthusiasts. Lou Clayton was an excellent golfer, and Redmond was continually boasting about the golfing ability of his hired entertainer until one night Duffy retorted that he knew a man who could beat Clayton. He said his man was Frankie Chester, who, besides being a great golfer, was one of the Silver Slipper's best customers.

Runyon described Chester as a crack amateur golfer, and a "high-rollin' fool who seemed to have plenty of potatoes, which he showered on café owners, the prize broads of the period, auto salesmen and other venders of luxury." A match was arranged, with everyone on Broadway taking sides, and backing their opinions with large bets. The game was played at dawn one day after Clayton was through working and Chester was through playing. But before the match began the Clayton group, to demonstrate their sportsmanship, offered to buy a round of drinks. No one dissented. It was then that someone gave Chester his first Mickey Finn. One Mickey would prevent the ordinary man from playing even a game of marbles. But apparently Chester was not of common clay. The players were ready to tee off on the first hole when one of the Clayton backers, disturbed because the drink seemed to have had no effect on Chester, suggested another round of drinks. There was mutual agreement on this idea, and Chester was slipped his second Mickey Finn.

Some people contend that the Geneva convention should have outlawed the administering of two Mickey Finns to one person in the same day, or at least declared a fiendish crime of this nature a misdemeanor. The fact that Chester beat Clayton that day by scoring 67 for eighteen holes caused so much amazement, especially among the Clayton men, that Damon later wrote a brief article recording the event to assure its place in history.

". . . Frankie stepped out and uncorked 67," Damon wrote. "I was on the verge of saying he shot a 67, but it

would be just like the printer to fumble at this critical point
and come up with a typographical error. Our hero was
heard to say once on his journey around the course that
the dame he was out with the night before must have been
a member of the Borgia family, otherwise he never complained.

"I always thought it was a good thing for Frankie he
had such a stout constitution. Another man might have
thought of dying and Frankie's backers were not citizens
who would have tolerated demise with their money at
stake."

7

BROADWAY FABLES

There is a story you can hear on Broadway if you find the right person, and he has some leisure time, and it is the right hour of night. The tale goes back to the fall of 1929 when the gloomy shadows of the depression were beginning to settle across the country. It had dimmed the spirit of the easy spenders along Broadway, many of whom then discovered that money, much to their chagrin, was not only the medium of exchange used in betting on a horse race or a prize fight, but was needed to obtain food and lodging. According to the story, it was at this time that Damon Runyon went to a doctor for a physical checkup. Damon worried a great deal about his health, and some even thought him a hypochondriac.

When the doctor had completed his examination, he told Damon to put on his clothes. The doctor began pacing around the room. Damon didn't like the expression on the physician's face.

"What's the verdict, Doc?" Damon asked.

"It's your appendix."

"Well, what about it?"

The doctor began pacing the room again. He lighted a cigarette. "It has to come out," he said, pronouncing each word slowly.

The blood drained slowly from Damon's face. Something in his stomach began spinning around like a merry-go-round out of control.

"You feel all right?" the doctor asked, surprised that his patient should have an attack so soon.

"No," Damon replied, "I never felt worse in my life."

"You're acting like a child," the doctor said. "There's nothing really to worry about. It'll be a comparatively simple operation. The percentage of people who die from appendicitis is no longer what it used to be."

"I know," Damon said, "what you say may be true, but only last week three of my friends went to the hospital to have their appendices taken out, and they were taken out feet first."

"Mere coincidences, my boy," the doctor said.

Damon walked over to the water cooler and drank a

glass of water. Then he drank a second glass. "Is this operation really necessary, doctor?"

"Most necessary." Both men were silent.

"All right," Damon said finally, "then I want the best
surgeon in the country to do it. I want to be in the best
hospital in the city with every precaution taken."

"Runyon," the doctor said with some impatience, "you're
a hypochondriac."

"I don't care what the hell I am. All I know is that I'm
much too handsome and talented to kick the bucket just
now. I want the best medical attention money can buy."

"It will be quite expensive."

"How much?"

"At least five hundred dollars."

Damon found a chair and slowly lowered himself into it.
This was a real blow. "Five hundred dollars," he whispered. "All I have in the bank is fifty. These are hard
times."

"You could go to Bellevue," the doctor suggested.

Damon stared at his doctor. Then he jumped to his feet,
put on his hat and coat, and walked to the door. "Start arranging everything just as I wanted it."

Damon hurried back to the Hotel Forrest, the story continues, rushed to his room and locked the door behind
him. He set his typewriter in the center of a table, placed a
pile of paper on one side of it and a carton of cigarettes on
the other. Two hours later he had smoked a package of
cigarettes and had thrown twelve pages of copy into the
wastepaper basket. He began again.

"What I always say is that Wilbur Willard is nothing
but a very lucky guy, because what is it but luck that has

him teetering along Forty-ninth Street one cold, snowy morning when Lillian is mee-owing around the sidewalk looking for her mama?"

The tale that follows is one of the most amusing short stories ever written about a cat. This was the first of Runyon's short stories which became known as Broadway fables. They made their author famous, and rich enough to pay for a dozen appendectomies if he needed them.

The stories are told by an engaging narrator who is never named but who is certainly well informed on all activities revolving about Fiftieth Street. He has all the qualities of a first-rate reporter: he is a good listener; his attitude toward Broadway and its people is completely objective; he never becomes emotionally enthusiastic; and in his opinion no one is completely good or bad. Although he professes to be greatly opposed to guys who break the law, his only companions seem to be criminals, gamblers, and bootleggers. His ability to fraternize with gangsters and at the same time to remain on friendly terms with the police is a major diplomatic feat. The narrator, who bears a striking resemblance to Damon Runyon, epitomizes the ideal of the innocent bystander. In employing a single narrator for his tales, Runyon created for himself a definite writing style and a structural pattern that neatly fitted all his story ideas.

In time it was only necessary for Damon to turn over his ideas to the narrator who would take the story from there.

Damon sent his first short story to the *Cosmopolitan Magazine*. A few days later he received a telephone call from Ray Long, who was then editor of the *Cosmopolitan*. Ray's voice was excited.

"Damon, that story was wonderful," he said.

"Stop kidding, Ray," Damon answered, "I'm in no mood to be kidded."

"It's just what we want, Damon, and a check for a thousand dollars is in the mail."

"What are you trying to do?" Damon demanded, almost dropping the phone. "Ruin my amateur standing?"

"Well, if a thousand dollars will do it," Long said, "I stand ready to accept anything you write at the same figure."

Along Broadway some will tell you that Runyon wrote this story because he needed the money for an appendectomy. Others will label it a pure fable. But since the history of Broadway is an interwinding pattern of legend and fact, the story will be told and retold until one day the person who challenges its authenticity will be castigated as an iconoclast. It is true, however, that Damon wrote the first of his famous short stories because he needed money. The depression that forced men with college degrees to sell apples on street corners inspired Damon to turn to fiction to supplement his newspaper salary.

Although short stories of Runyon's had appeared before this time, none of them are remembered today. While he was a reporter in Denver he sold fiction to *Harper's Weekly*, the *Century*, the *Metropolitan*, *Hampton's Magazine*, and other national magazines, besides the work he did, when he first came to New York, in collaboration with Charles Van Loan. The money they made on the sale of their stories was divided equally between them, but Van Loan's name appeared as the author of all the stories.

Later Damon made a similar arrangement with Irvin S. Cobb, furnishing the plots for some of Cobb's stories, and receiving an equal share of the financial rewards.

For years Damon's friends had been urging him to turn out short stories. They insisted that his style of placing one little word after another was made to order for fiction writing. Damon would listen courteously, shake his head, and reply with his stock answer: "I can't write that stuff. I wouldn't know where to start." Yet, Damon's short stories were almost immediately successful, and his friends returned to remind him that they had been counseling him to write fiction for a long time.

"I told you so, Damon," a friend usually said on these occasions. "Why did you wait so long before you began turning out short stories?"

"I was building up background," Damon invariably replied.

Of all Damon's friends, Winchell was the most persistent in goading him into writing short stories. He made it his particular task to supply Runyon with self-confidence. Winchell is at his best when he's giving some friend a pep talk, and after a session with the columnist, Runyon had enough faith in himself to lick the world. There were times after Runyon had started on this new venture when he lost confidence, complaining that his talent was a lie, or his material a stockpile of triteness. When this happened, Winchell was always ready to rekindle Damon's creative ambitions. Perhaps in recognition of Winchell's faith in his writing, Damon had Winchell play a leading role in one of his early stories, "Romance in the Roaring Forties."

"Only a rank sucker will think of taking two peeks at Dave the Dude's doll," the story begins, "because while

Dave may stand for the first peek, figuring it is a mistake, it
is a sure thing he will get sored up at the second peek, and
Dave the Dude is certainly not a man to have sored up at
you.

"But this Waldo Winchester is one hundred per cent
sucker, which is why he takes quite a number of peeks at
Dave's doll. And what is more, she takes quite a number
of peeks right back at him. And there you are. When a guy
and a doll get to taking peeks back and forth at each other,
why, there you are indeed.

"This Waldo Winchester is a nice-looking young guy
who writes pieces about Broadway for the *Morning Item.*
He writes about the goings-on in night clubs, such as fights,
and one thing and another, and also about who is running
around with who, including guys and dolls.

"Sometimes this is very embarrassing to people who
may be married and are running around with people who
are not married, but of course Waldo Winchester cannot
be expected to ask one and all for their marriage certificates
before he writes his pieces for the paper."

Waldo Winchester is hardly the hero of this story, for he
is pushed around considerably by the other characters,
which is something that seldom happens to Winchell in
real life. First, Dave the Dude knocks Waldo Winchester
"bowlegged" when he finds the columnist and Miss Billy
Perry "kissing each other back and forth friendly." Later,
when Dave the Dude discovers that his girl is in love with
Waldo Winchester, he arranges a big wedding, buys a ring,
and plans to set the couple up in the housekeeping
business.

It develops, however, that Waldo Winchester is married

to Lola Sapola, an acrobat, who is described as being four feet high and five feet wide, and has a face that resembles a full moon and is as wide as her shoulders. But since Dave the Dude is ignorant of this fact, the wedding begins as scheduled. In describing Waldo Winchester as he reluctantly makes his way to the altar, the narrator of the story remarks: "I once see two guys go to the old warm squativoo up in Sing Sing, and I wish to say both are laughing heartily compared to Waldo Winchester at this moment." At the last moment Lola breaks in on the scene, floors Dave the Dude with a few well-directed punches, and goes off with Waldo slung over her shoulder. The wedding ceremony continues despite the interruptions when Miss Billy Perry suddenly realizes she has been in love with Dave the Dude all the time.

This is the pattern of many of Runyon's stories: a problem arises, which, if it is not immediately solved, will result in a dire calamity for a newspaper columnist, some doll, an old woman, a child, a gambler, or a gangster. The critical issues are always resolved in an unusual and bizarre fashion, and frequently it is necessary to resort to a few homicides to bring the story to a happy conclusion. Runyon never finds it necessary to bring a murderer to justice, and if the crime is committed in a good cause, the gunman is rewarded for his deed. The stories usually have a happy ending, but always with cynical qualifications. At the end of "Romance in the Roaring Forties," the narrator relates:

"I see Mr. and Mrs. Dave the Dude the other day, and they seem very happy. But you never can tell about married people, so of course I am never going to let on to Dave the Dude that I am the one who telephones Lola Sapola at the Marx Hotel, because maybe I do not do Dave any too much of a favor, at that."

One of the most justified murders occurs in "The Lily of St. Pierre" when Jack O'Hearts kills Louie the Lug in Good Time Charley Bernstein's. Some of the boys, including the narrator, are offended by Jack O'Hearts' action because Louie the Lug is the tenor in the quartet that sings at Good Time Charley's. ". . . we sing 'I Can't Give You Anything but Love, Baby,' which is a very fine song for quartet singing," the narrator explains, "especially when you have a guy singing a nice bass, such as Good Time Charley, who can come in on every line with a bug bum-bum, like this:

I can't give you anything but luh-huh-vuh,
Bay-hay-bee!
BUM-BUM!

"I am the one who holds these last words, such as love, and baby, and you can hear my fine baritone very far indeed, especially when I give a little extra roll like bay-hay-ay-ay-BEE! Then when Good Time Charley comes in with his old bum-bum, it is worth going a long way to hear."

Jack O'Hearts' explanation of why he killed Louie the Lug makes one of Runyon's most sentimental stories. Jack O'Hearts became ill with pneumonia while in St. Pierre, Newfoundland, on rum-running business. A kind village doctor and his granddaughter, Lily, nursed him back to health. Jack O'Hearts grew very fond of Lily and the doctor and returned to St. Pierre often to visit them on his vacations. Louie the Lug accompanied Jack on one of these trips, and although Jack did not notice it, Louie paid a good deal of attention to Lily, who had grown into woman-hood. Sometime later, when he returned to the United States, Jack learned that Louie had persuaded Lily to run away with him, and had then abandoned her when she developed tuberculosis. Jack found Lily in a hospital, and when she died he took her back to St. Pierre for burial. Then he returned to search for Louie the Lug.

After Jack O'Hearts apologizes to the Broadway boys for killing the tenor in their quartet, he points out that he is a fine tenor himself, and offers to take Louie the Lug's place. Runyon has woven a fine thread of sadness into this tale, but he would never destroy the pattern of his stories by permitting one of them to end in a sentimental key. All events must be viewed with realistic indifference. "The Lily of St. Pierre" ends with this observation:

"Personally I do not think Jack's tenor is as good as Louie the Lug's, especially when it comes to hitting the very high notes in such songs as Sweet Adeline, because he does not hold them long enough to let Good Time Charley in with his bum-bum.

"But of course this does not go if Jack O'Hearts hears it, as I am never sure he does not clip Louie the Lug just to get a place in our quartet, at that."

To write his stories Runyon merely opened his imagina-tion and let the life of Broadway stroll through. He care-fully selected the personalities he desired, dressed them into the characters he needed, supplied all the male mem-bers with guns, gave them all appropriate monikers, and allowed them to speak in their native tongue. He appropriated the names of his characters from real life, some-times, altered others, and invented the rest. His real-life models were often gamblers and gunmen whom any competent New York detective could recognize, and at other times Damon sidetracked law-abiding friends into slightly illegal fictional activities.

Harry the Horse, Little Isadore, and Spanish John are natives of Brooklyn, where they are regarded as disreputable neighbors by the other residents. ". . . many citizens of Brooklyn will be very glad indeed to see Harry the Horse, Little Isadore and Spanish John move away from there," according to the report in one of the stories, "as they are always doing something that is considered a knock to the community, such as robbing people, or maybe shooting or stabbing them, and throwing pineapples, and carrying on generally."

Judge Goldfobber is said to be a "wonderful hand for keeping citizens from getting into the sneezer [jail], and better than Houdini when it comes to getting them out of the sneezer after they are in." Educated Edmund is called Educated Edmund because "he once goes to Erasmus High School and is considered a very fine scholar, indeed . . ." Miss Missouri Martin, who runs the Three Hundred Club, "tells everything she knows as soon as she knows it, which is very often before it happens." Dream Street Rose is a short, thick-set, square-looking old doll, with a square pan and square shoulders, and she's as strong and lively as Jim Londos, the wrestler. "In fact, Jim Londos will never be any better than 6 to 5 in my line over Dream Street Rose, if she is in any kind of shape." Angie the Ox is an importer of fine liquors, besides enjoying a splendid trade in other lines, "including artichokes and extortion."

The Louse Kid has a very weak face, but is supposed to be "a wonderful hand with a burlap bag when anybody wishes to put somebody in such a bag, which is considered a great practical joke in Brooklyn . . ." Rusty Charley is probably the toughest member of the cast, which includes some extremely sturdy individuals. "In fact, this Rusty Charley is what is called a gorill, because he is known to often carry a gun in his pants pocket, and sometimes to shoot people down as dead as door-nails with it if he does not like the way they wear their hats—and Rusty Charley is very critical of hats. The chances are Rusty Charley shoots many a guy in this man's town, and those he does not shoot he sticks with his shiv—which is a knife—and the only reason he is not in jail is because he just gets out of it, and the law does not have time to think up something to put him back in again for."

Regret earned his name because "it seems he wins a very large bet the year the Whitney filly, Regret, grabs the Kentucky Derby, and can never forget it, which is maybe because it is the only very large bet he ever wins in his life." John Wangle is so thin he must be "two pounds lighter than a stack of wheats." One character is called Izzy Cheesecake because he frequents delicatessen stores where he always eats cheesecake. Jo-jo has jowls you can cut steaks off of, and sleepy eyes, and "he sometimes reminds me of an old lion I once seen in a cage in Ringling's circus." There are many more—Sam the Gonoph, Benny South Street, Liverlips, The Brain, Feet Samuels, who has feet like violin cases, Rochester Red, the Pale Face Kid,

Big Jule, Hot Horse Herbie, Joe the Joker, a clever dispenser of the hot foot, Frankie Ferocious, an efficient administrator in the murder business, Hymie Banjo Eyes, Dancing Dan, Last Card Louie, Big Nig, and Nick the Greek.

These are the characters who people Runyon's stories. It is obvious that their activities will be stimulating, perhaps vulgar at times, but never conventional or subtle. When a person reads of their crimes in a newspaper, he usually becomes angry at their lawlessness and then disgusted with their misled lives. But in a Runyon story their felonies are magically transformed into amusing adventures; their immorality becomes the spice that brings the high taste of laughter to almost every page. Runyon employs his language like a skilled musician, regulating the pattern of his work carefully so that the tones of comedy and pathos are clear, resonant, and effective.

Runyon's stories brought a new and colorful jargon to the attention of the public. Damon said he had merely recorded the argot he heard along Broadway and was not responsible for any innovations in the American language. In his short-story world all men and women are "guys" and "dolls," a worn-out race horse is described as being "practically mucilage," a doughty individual has "plenty of ticker," a person who owns a grocery store is in the "grocery dodge," a man whose blood pressure is "away up in the paint cards" has high blood pressure, and a "boat-race" is a horse race in which the winner has been dishonestly selected beforehand, while a "tank job" is a prize fight that has been fixed.

Two of the most important nouns in the Runyon stories

are "money" and "gun," although these particular words are never used. A gun, either a revolver or an automatic, is a "rod," a "John Roscoe," or an "equalizer." "Equalizer" is the more original and picturesque term, and on every other page of most stories one of the characters "outs with the old equalizer." This usually makes the situation equal in favor of the possessor of the equalizer. Money is referred to as "potatoes" or "scratch.' The denominational terms used are a G for a thousand dollars; a "finnif," a "fin," or a "pound note," five dollars; a "deuce," two dollars; and a "buck" or a "bob," one dollar.

Mindy's restaurant, and Good Time Charley's Speakeasy are the settings for most of the tales. The action either begins or ends at one of these spots, and frequently the main character relates the story to the narrator while the latter is eating a dish of Mindy's cold borscht. Mindy's is Lindy's, and other than changing one letter of the name, Runyon made no attempt to disguise the Broadway restaurant. Good Time Charley Bernstein, a well-liked character, has his liquor dispensary in West Forty-seventh Street. Some very libelous statements are made about Good Time Charley's liquor. "I never drink anything that is sold in Good Time Charley's, as a personal favor to Charley," the narrator states at one point. "He says he wishes to retain my friendship." After his place is raided by G-men, Charley becomes an avid reader of the obituary notices in the newspapers. "Charley figures that some of the G-guys may be tempted to take a belt or two at the merchandise they confiscate, and Charley says if they do he is even with them for life."

One of the best descriptions of Runyon's New York is

found in "Dream Street Rose." The block of Forty-seventh Street between Sixth and Seventh Avenues is called Dream Street.

"In Dream Street there are many theatrical hotels, and rooming houses, and restaurants, and speaks, including Good Time Charley's Gingham Shoppe, and in the summer time the characters I mention sit on the stoops or lean against the railings along Dream Street, and the gab you hear sometimes sounds very dreamy indeed. In fact, it sometimes sounds very pipe-dreamy.

"Many actors, male and female, and especially vaudeville actors, live in the hotels and rooming houses, and vaudeville actors, both male and female, are great hands for sitting around dreaming out loud about how they will practically assassinate the public in the Palace if ever they get a chance.

"Furthermore, in Dream Street are always many hand-bookies and horse players, who sit on the church steps on the cool side of Dream Street in the summer and dream about big killings on the races, and there are also nearly always many fight managers, and sometimes fighters, hanging out in front of the restaurants, picking their teeth and dreaming about winning championships of the world, although up to this time no champion of the world has yet come out of Dream Street.

"In this street you see burlesque dolls, and hoofers, and guys who write songs, and saxophone players, and newsboys, and newspaper scribes, and taxi drivers, and blind guys, and midgets, and blondes with Pomeranian pooches, or maybe French poodles, and guys with whiskers, and night-club entertainers, and I do not know what all else.

And all of these characters are interesting to look at, and some of them are very interesting to talk to, although if you listen to several I know long enough, you may get the idea that they are somewhat daffy, especially the horse players.

"But personally I consider all horse players more or less daffy anyway. In fact, the way I look at it, if a guy is not daffy he will not be playing the horses."

Every Broadway dweller has at least one tale to tell: a fragment of his or her life that has a special significance; an incident that by a touch of comedy or a moment of pathos is lifted from the ordinary context of happenings. These become the basic ingredients of Runyon's plots. "Butch Minds the Baby" is the story of Big Butch, a safe-cracker who quits his profession because one more conviction will send him to jail for life. He reforms, marries, and has a baby. One night Harry the Horse offers him $10,000 if he will open one last safe for the boys from Brooklyn. Big Butch is willing, but on that particular night he has to mind the baby because his wife is attending a wake in the Bronx. This problem is solved when Big Butch agrees to bring the baby along on the job. While Big Butch is working on the safe, the baby, John Ignatius, Junior, plays with his father's tools, drinks a bottle of milk, and is greatly amused by the loud noise when Big Butch blows the safe open. When Big Butch is leaving the scene of the crime, the police surround him, but when the police sergeant sees John Ignatius, Junior, he scolds the patrolman for suspecting that a man with a baby in his arms would be out cracking safes.

Abe Bronson, a former policeman, who is now a reigning

Broadway regular, gave Runyon the foundation for "Butch Minds the Baby." "I had this three-room apartment here on the West Side," Abe explains, when relating how Damon transplanted him into fiction as Big Butch, "and a little gal I know got put out of her hotel for chronic non-payment of the rent, so she went out to Hollywood and all she got out of that was a baby but no permanent man. So she came back two years later with this kid, eight weeks old, and she goes back to the hotel, but they know her from the last time and put her out again first time she fails to make with the moola.

"So I tell her to come on over and live in one room of my three-room place, because two rooms are all I need. She says, 'What about the rent money?' And I say, 'Come on in. It ain't costing. I can't pay the rent neither.' So she moved with the baby, and that night she went out and came home drunk. She wanted to pick up the baby and I told her not to, because she would sure hurt the kid bad, or drop it or kill it in her condition.

"She wouldn't pay any attention, but kept grabbing at the baby, and when I made her stop she started to fight me. I gave her a slap in the kisser and she went out and got blind and stayed away three days. I had the baby to take care of. I made the formula and changed its diaper and did the washing and everything.

"That little baby boy was the most beautiful thing you ever laid eyes on. I was nuts about the kid. He had eyes like deep blue sapphires. I think he liked me too. Anyhow, he never yelled once, and he used to scream all the time whenever his mother touched him.

"Those days I was taking care of him, I had to go out to

eat once in a while, and I went to Lindy's and told Mrs.
Lindy what a shame it was about the poor kid. So Mrs.
Lindy told Damon, and the three of us fixed a way to take
care of the baby and get him taken out to his grandfather
in Oakland, and a deal was drawn up so that the mother
didn't get him and hurt him."

Butch Tower and Sam Boston are the sources for "Hold
'Em, Yale!" and Phocian Howard was the hero of "All
Horse Players Die Broke."

Although the characters in Runyon stories are seldom
on the side of the law, they are further divided into bad
guys and good guys when they enter one of his tales.
Every story must have a hero and a villain no matter how
questionable the qualifications of the hero may be. The
heroes in Runyon stories usually make use of their illicit
talents to come to the aid of a doll, either young or old,
who is in trouble, or will be in trouble unless some drastic
action is taken. Drastic is the middle name of all Runyon
characters. There are instances when the lives of criminals
are spared because they have performed a good deed.
One Christmas Eve two gunmen hunting Dancing Dan
do not recognize him when he leaves Good Time Charley's
because he has dressed himself in a Santa Claus suit and
is on his way to fill an old lady's stocking with jewelry.
This is "Dancing Dan's Christmas."

In discussing Runyon's writing formula, which sometimes mystified the critics because it was so successful,
J. C. Furnas, the author and critic, wrote, "Almost invariably the fundamental principle is the reasonably well-
worn device of making a hard-boiled enemy of society be-
have like St. Francis of Assisi, demonstrating for all and

sundry that the softest hearts may be found beneath the
latest fashion in bullet-proof vests."

Robert Van Gelder, book critic for the *New York Times,*
seemed to see a similarity between Runyon's plots and the
plot of "Snow White and the Seven Dwarfs." He mentioned his theory to Runyon one day. "I have been reading
the stories for a dozen years," Van Gelder said, "and it has
seemed to me that although sometimes the main character
is a gangster who has been shot and is looking for a quiet
place to die, or a chorus girl whose back has been broken
by a Broadway bully, or a horse player who has not been
hitting them and is looking for a doll with some potatoes,
this main character always is Snow White. And though
this main character may be helped out of his or her horrible
predicament by a thief or a murder-for-hire or an old lush
of an apple woman, the helper has a lot in common with
the dwarfs."

Runyon listened attentively, nodding his head in agreement as the critic spoke. When Van Gelder stopped,
Damon considered his remarks a moment. "I have one
amendment to make to add to your analysis," he said.
"Sometimes the main character is Cinderella."

It was the English who first called Runyon a new force
in American fiction, and felt no scruples about placing him
in the ranks of the great creators of English literature.
Lord Beaverbrook, the publisher, bought the English
rights to *More Than Somewhat,* a collection of Runyon's
short stories, and ran one story a day in the *Evening
Standard* as a centerfold spread with accompanying wood-
cut illustrations of the British conception of American
gangsters. Some readers complained that Runyon stories

violated the king's English and weren't fit for publication in a London newspaper, while others compared Runyon to Shakespeare, Milton, Dickens, and Thomas Hardy.

One English critic said Runyon had created a humanity "as new and as startling as that invented by Lewis Carroll in *Alice in Wonderland.*" Another remarked, "Seriously, though in a minor sphere, Runyon is comparable to Shakespeare and Milton as an improvisator of language. Runyon should be rated a genius for breaking so much new ground." But not every Englishman was willing to accept Runyon as cordially as did the critics. One reader wrote a letter to the Beaverbrook paper after it had begun printing Runyon stories. "For the love of Mike, stop it," he pleaded. "Some American slang is amusing, some is simply putrid. Runyon's is the latter variety. This miserable stuff has such an unpleasant effect on my nervous system that I now carefully avoid opening my *Evening Standard* lest I should see Runyon in it."

During the '30's most of England was reading Runyon and adopting Runyonese into the language. At the height of Runyon's popularity there, Gilbert Miller, the American producer, was dining with an Englishman who was heir to a high-ranking title. The Englishman's father had only recently died, and Miller was unaware of his death.

"What do you think happened?" asked the heir.

"I don't know," replied Miller. "What has happened?"

The heir adjusted his monocle and said, "The pater has cooled."

The English took their Runyon vogue seriously, and in writing the introduction to an English edition of the Runyon short-story collection, E. C. Bentley, the London critic, attempted what was really the first complete critique of the Runyon works. In his introduction to *The Best of Runyon,* Mr. Bentley wrote:

"Before Damon Runyon began writing his stories of the bandits of Broadway, he had made himself a national reputation in America as a newspaper-man, a descriptive reporter who could deal with any event in the day's doings, from a horse-race at Miami to an electrocution at Ossining, in a manner that put him in a class by himself. . . . He broke into literature, quite suddenly, with a hilarious short story of the gangsters and crooks infesting a certain section of Broadway, the main artery of New York's life—the Hardened Artery, as Walter Winchell has called it. He followed it up with many others of the same sort; all of them, in fact, told by the same imaginary narrator, and told in a tone and a language that make up one of the richest contributions to comic literature in our time."

Bentley considered Runyon unique. He said he did not expect any other writer in the future to make crime, violence, dissipation, and predatory worthlessness, together with occasional offhand decency where you would least expect it, as keenly interesting and as frantically funny as Damon Runyon does.

"You cannot help liking his guys and dolls," he wrote. "I do not mean that they—the guys, anyway—would be nice to know, or even safe. In fact, if it is left to me, I will as soon go in bathing with a school of sharks, or maybe sooner. (I am sorry, but I find it impossible not to drift into Runyonese when writing of the creatures of his brain.) I do not mean that they are unselfish, good-hearted, high-minded guys and dolls. I do not mean that you will shed

tears when Angie the Ox gets cooled off by Lance Mc-
Gowan, or when Joey Perhaps gets what is coming to him
from Ollie Ortega, which is a short knife in the throat, or
when The Brain gets carved up quite some, and finally
hauls off and dies. I merely mean that they have a reckless,
courageous vitality that makes you like hearing about
them; that is, if you are an ordinary human being, such as
has always liked hearing about desperadoes."

Bentley is fascinated by the continuous use of the present tense in Runyon's stories, and the almost exclusive em-
ployment of a conversational style.

"They are all talk," he said, "the talk of the guy who is
telling them, or of other guys as reported by him. For
English readers, I suppose, the most curious thing about
that guy's talk will be his resolute avoidance of the past
tense, the remarkable things he does with the historic
present. The same thing is known in our own vulgar
tongue, of course; but it is incidental, and apt to take a
debased form—for example, 'So I says to him, "Did you
hear what I said?"' In Runyonese this would be, 'So I say
to him, "Do you hear what I say?"' Runyon's guy will say,
'About three weeks ago, Big Nig is down taking the waters
in Hot Springs, and anything else there may be to take in
Hot Springs.' He will not say, 'When I heard Bugs Lonigan
say this, I wished I had never been born'; he will say,
'When I hear Bugs Lonigan say this, I wish I am never
born.' There is a sort of ungrammatical purity about it,
an almost religious exactitude, that to me, at least, has
the strongest appeal. In all the Runyon stories, as published in America, I have found only one single instance
of a verb in the past tense."

Bentley shows a great deal of interest in the narrator, who is responsible for giving the stories their continuity, and devotes a part of his introduction to analyzing his personality.

"He does not give himself a name at any time, but it will do no harm to call him X," Mr. Bentley writes. "In some ways X is a strange guy to be mobbed up with such characters as he tells about. He is a nervous guy, for one thing; and even more remarkable, in the circumstances, than his nervousness, is his passion for respectability. He is 'greatly opposed to guys who violate the law,' as he insists again and again; and he can think of a million things he will rather do than be seen in the company of such guys. But as he is, on his own showing, practically never in any other kind of society, he must spend a harassing time. The truth is, X is very far from being one of the high shots, but is simply known to one and all as a guy who is just around. In fact, they figure him as harmless as a bag of marshmallows. Just the same, X is well known to every wrong gee on Broadway; and if one of them sees him and gives him a huge hello, what can X do? It would be very unsafe indeed if X tried playing the chill for such a guy."

Once Damon began writing fiction he had little difficulty marketing his stories. When magazine publishers learned that the sales of any issue containing a Runyon tale increased by as many as 60,000 copies, they beat a path to his door, competing with one another for his stories. He was soon receiving $5000 for a single short story. Hollywood discovered that the Runyon stories could be expanded into successful movies that multiplied box-office receipts. With this touchstone to guide their decisions, the movie producers purchased more than twenty Runyon stories. Meanwhile, collections of the Broadway tales were being published in book form. *Guys and Dolls* appeared in 1931; *Blue Plate Special,* 1934; *Money from Home,* 1935; *The Best of Runyon* and *Take It Easy* both appeared in 1938. Later collections were *Damon Runyon Favorites,* which was published in 1942, and *Runyon à la Carte,* in 1944.

This excited activity on the part of editors, publishers, and producers over his writings greatly enhanced the reputation of his pocketbook. This was money; and Damon had been seeking money all his life. He began eating, gambling, and dressing in a manner that in his mind was equal to pleasure. Damon always gave Broadway credit for his good fortune. He once remarked, "I took one little section of New York and made half a million writing about it."

One night he accompanied a cameraman who had set up his equipment on top of the Trans-Lux Theatre's marquee in order to photograph the Times Square area. For a time they looked on the scene where Broadway and Seventh Avenue merge into a single stream of white and yellow lights flowing against the solid banks of theaters, hotels, drugstores, fruit-juice and hot-dog stands, novelty shops, taverns, and arcadiums. The cameraman nudged Damon. "I bet we're looking on the most expensive strip of real estate in the world," he said.

"Why, that's nothing," Damon countered. "I've earned more money from this street than the people who own the real estate on it." Either Damon was exaggerating to impress the cameraman, or his original estimate of having made half a million writing about Broadway was much too low.

Working as a reporter for a newspaper Damon was able to manufacture as many as 6000 words a day. When he first began writing fiction he was dismayed by the fact that it took from two to four days of hard work to complete one short story of about 4000 words. Creating the easy, fluid style that seemed to be an inherent quality of his stories was a deliberate and laborious task for Damon. Sitting before his typewriter at the beginning of a story, Damon was tense and nervous, like a prize fighter waiting in his corner for the first round. He had little patience with the first drafts of his story and revised them continually. When he became angry with the development of a tale as it formed on the paper before him, he would rip the page from the typewriter and, with a dramatic gesture, properly accompanied by an invocation of profanity, would tear the page into countless pieces. He estimated that he often wrote 20,000 words before he had 4000 that pleased him.

But like most reporters who habitually work in noisy press boxes or city rooms, Damon had uncommon powers of concentration. He liked to have people around him during the hours that he was awake, and his hotel suite was often crowded with friends, touts, sightseers, and freeloaders. But whenever an idea began to expand into a plot and took tentative steps toward developing into a story, Damon left his company. He went into an adjoining room, closed the door behind him, and went to work. The world on the other side of the door was completely blanked out of his consciousness.

Damon Runyon was now known as a short-story writer,

but he still considered himself a newspaper reporter. The city room was his home; going out on the street to cover a news event and writing to beat a deadline was the great adventure Damon found in life. When he was out of town on a big story that extended over several weeks, Damon refused to lessen the pace. Other reporters might rest on the week end, but Runyon kept busy. It was part of his routine when out of the city to call the desk on Saturday afternoon. "This is Runyon," he usually reported. "I'll file a fresh story for you tomorrow for the first edition Monday. Any instructions?" No matter who answered the telephone, the city editor, assistant city editor, or the head copy boy, he always asked for instruction.

Runyon's friends were puzzled by the fact that he continued as a Hearst newspaperman after the success of his short stories made it possible for him to be financially independent of the routine and grind of a steady job. But Runyon had his own reasons for keeping his job.

"Now that you're batting out fiction for that big dough," Louis Sobol, the columnist, once said to Runyon, "I guess you'll be quitting the newspaper grind."

"If I gave up a steady job," Runyon said, "I'd be writing for scared money. It's like playing poker with scared dough—you usually lose."

Runyon took one turn at the theater. He collaborated with Howard Lindsay in writing *A Slight Case of Murder*, which Lindsay produced in the fall of 1935. The play concerns the hectic movements of the usual assortment of Runyon thugs, touts, racketeers, and politicians during the August racing season at Saratoga. When a former bootlegger, attempting to sell beer legitimately after the repeal of prohibition, visits his Saratoga home during the racing season, he finds four slain gunmen resting in the house. A high point in the play comes when the reformed racketeer decides to dispose of the bodies by leaving them on the doorsteps of four friends. Apparently the theater critics were not acquainted with the Runyon short stories, because the unconventional shenanigans in the play bewildered them to such an extent that they couldn't enjoy themselves.

Reviewing the play for the *Evening Journal,* John Anderson said, "It gave, now and then, as its actors ran hither and yon, a faint suggestion that its movement has been patterned on the commuting hour in the Grand Central Depot, but its lines always save it."

Percy Hammond, writing in the *N. Y. Herald Tribune,* said, "As a drama lover who believes nearly everything he sees and hears in the theatre, I was a bit discomforted by the careless disposition of the bodies of the slightly murdered men—this, I thought, was going too far with my credulity. But it was done with such blithely humorous disregard of dramatic ethics that I enjoyed its impudence while deploring its—shall I say—technique."

Runyon said the play was only "mediumly-funny." At any rate, Hollywood bought the rights and made the play into a movie without changing the title. This confused the movie fans. Some people complained that it wasn't in the American or Hollywood tradition to call a movie *A Slight Case of Murder*. It should have been immense, brilliant, or sensational, they argued.

No matter what the critics said of his fiction writing, Damon believed he had received the highest accolade as a

newspaperman. Arthur Brisbane, the renowned Hearst
editor and columnist, once said, "Runyon is the best reporter in the world." This verdict made Damon proud and
happy, for this was the goal he had been seeking; all other
success was superficial. "It was undeserved," Damon said,
when he was told of Brisbane's remark, "but it is the nicest
thing ever said about me." Brisbane died in 1936, and
Hearst began searching for a new columnist. Runyon was
writing a column called "Both Barrels" for the sports section of the *American* at the time. Hearst asked Runyon to
abandon sports and write a general column for the King
Features Syndicate. Runyon's new column, called "As I
See It," began appearing in January 1937, and was syndicated in sixteen Hearst papers. For a time Runyon tried
his hand at writing serious, editorial columns in the Brisbane vein, but he soon realized that his style and temperament was not suitable for playing the role of the pundit.
Hearst changed the name of the column to "The Brighter
Side" and told Runyon that people were tired of egotistical
columnists who were always finding fault and trying to
run the world with a typewriter. He said he wanted Runyon to amuse people. Runyon's column was thereafter
guided by these instructions. "You know," Runyon remarked, "a piece I wrote about canary birds got more
responses than anything I could write about a real serious
subject. You'd be surprised how many men own canary
birds."

His column became a hock shop of items that pleased
Damon's fancy, ranging from dissertations on Broadway
characters to dogs and cats, to dieting women, to remi-
niscing on sports. Damon's columns supplied the material

for three books. Whenever he wished to regale his readers with philosophy, he wrote a My-Old-Man-used-to-say column. Damon's Old Man had something to say on love, matrimony, parents, cooking and food, sinners, preachers, growing old, suicide, doctors, male gossips, lady sports, nice fellows, liars, and, in fact, on every subject that might have been touched upon in a conversation in the saloons of his old home town of Pueblo. These articles were designed as light entertainment, but they also had an undercurrent of seriousness. Their principal theme was the presentation of the salient arguments in favor of the other side of the question. Damon's Old Man had a penchant for examining the other side of problems that were universally considered to have only one side.

In 1939 a compilation of thirty-five of these articles was published in a book called *My Old Man.* Damon also created a winsome Brooklyn husband, Joe Turp, who wrote letters to Runyon concerning the feminine inconsistencies of his wife, Ethel, and related, in some detail, the trials, tribulations, and joys of domestic life in Brooklyn. The Joe Turp letters were the substance of another book, *My Wife Ethel,* which was published in 1940. Joe and Ethel Turp were also the basis of a radio show that was done by those noted vaudevillians, Block and Sully, and was heard for a time over Station WMCA. In 1946, *Short Takes,* a collection of the readers' choice of Runyon's best columns, was published.

A woman wrote Runyon that she thought his column the best in the world. Damon was pleased and acknowledged receipt of the letter in his column.

"Well, it ought to be [the best column in the world] in

view of the many years I have been stealing from the greatest writers that ever lived to entertain and instruct my parishioners.

"I tell you, dearly beloved, that at times my efforts in intellectual larceny in your behalf have been positively superhuman. I do not say my column would be more than just real good if I relied entirely upon my own noodle, but with centuries of writing to prowl through, and pick and choose from, I would be a poor stick, indeed, did I not make it the best.

"Sometimes I wonder if youse appreciate me.

"I steal from Plato, Socrates, Woodrow Wilson, Shakespeare, Montaigne, Mr. Dooley, Euripides, Nat Fleisher's All-Time Ring Record, Lincoln's speeches, Ingersoll's lectures, LaGuardia's readings of the comic strips, Caesar (Irving and Arthur and Julius), Butler (Nick, Sam, Ben and Bill), Dickens, Cato, Thoreau, Emerson and Whitman.

"I steal from Dante, Goethe, Aesop, Confucius, Karl Marx, Yussel Stalin, Conrad, James G. Blaine, Demosthenes, Sheridan (Dick and Phil), Disraeli, Nick the Greek, Joe Louis, Bob Fitzsimmons, Hans Christian Andersen, Grimm, L. B. Mayer, Henry Mencken, Good Time Charley, George Jean Nathan, George Washington, Grover Cleveland, Clay, Calhoun, Talleyrand, Thomas Paine."

One of Damon's most-treasured literary sources was the newspaper writer Brann, the Iconoclast. To protect himself, Damon said he followed certain rules in his literary pilfering, generally being careful not to steal from anyone who had not been dead for many years.

Damon didn't fear any legal penalty would result from his plagiarism. "It is simply that personally I do not fancy

being caught at my larceny lest my own erudition thereafter be suspect," he wrote. "I mean I do not like to en-
counter glances that tell me that the glancer is saying to
himself, this Runyon is an intellectual gonniff."

From long experience Damon learned that it was best
to steal from the classics which, though they are always
spoken of quite favorably in our best intellectual circles,
are seldom read. He pointed out that by making slight
revisions in the great works a person could pass off this
wisdom as being his own and acquire the reputation of
being an educated fellow.

Damon's intention was not to enhance his own reputation but to serve his readers. "I would like to see another
column that presents as great a variety of brains burglary
as this," he wrote. "Other columnists steal from a limited
number of sources and with great timidity. I steal from
everybody and as bold as brass. And yet I feel that in
depredations I am a sort of an intellectual Robin Hood.
I steal from the rich in wisdom and give it to the poor,
if the members of my congregation will pardon the simile."

Runyon also contended that he made a practice of fore-
going his column when he had nothing to say. "I want to
say something as much as any man alive," he once remarked, "yet I have a feeling that whatever I say it
should be interesting or entertaining." Damon was carry-
out Mr. Hearst's instructions to amuse people.

In explaining his position, Damon wrote, "The man
never lived who had something to say every day of his
life. By something to say, I mean of course, something
worth listening to or reading. But if editors took to leaving
out columnists when they have nothing to say, every

columnist would be reduced to about three appearances per week and some less and that would be bad for the columning racket."

Damon was obsessed with a fear that he was overwriting his columns and trying the patience of his readers with unnecessary verbiage. After inspecting several of them, he found that they averaged 950 words per column, which was 200 words more than he was scheduled to write. This irritated his newspaper sense, which demanded terse and trenchant writing. He made a public confession of his sin in one of his columns. "I said to myself, Runyon, who do you think you are anyway, sounding your bazoo to that extent? I said, read those columns over again line by line and word by word, a harsh penalty to be sure, but justified by your breaking of the vow you took several years ago not to exceed 750 words per column, and see for yourself the amount of verbiage you got in.

"Well, that is just what I did and in every column I found enough of what I might call 'water' in the way of words to fill a vat. If this 'water' had been squeezed out no one of the columns would have exceeded 700 words and would have said everything I intended and probably better than it appeared with the excess.

"I found far too many 'buts' which seems to be a favorite word of mine, too many 'howevers,' too many 'wells' and 'in any events,' and too many 'of courses' and 'as I was sayings.' There was plenty of tautology, which is unnecessary repetition whether in word or in sense.

"How does this happen, you ask?

"Well (see, there it is!) in writing a column one word leads to another. You get to galloping along a certain line of thought and at the point where instinct tells you to pull up, something else occurs to your mind and you slide it in, hoping that they will somehow be able to stretch the space allotted you and make room for the excess.

"The copy reader probably cuts it out and you are always surprised that the amputation in no wise disturbs the continuity or thought of your essay, in fact, if you write a column for enough years you will learn that nothing the editor does to it affects the destiny of mankind or the course of the world."

Runyon had a habit of punctuating his column with Yiddish words. It was a stylistic trick that was dear to his heart. He was fond of words like "Nu?" (What's up?), "schlemiel" (dope), "nasher" (continuous eater of choice morsels), "trumbinich" (wise guy), "mishmash" (a hodge-podge), "tzimis" (making an issue of a minor thing), "Hock mir nisht kine chine-ik" (Don't bother me), "yold" (idiot), "bubbemeise" (old wives' tale, or any long-drawn-out story), "lochenkopf" (hole-in-the-head), and the "emmes" (the truth).

After his column began appearing in 1936 the output of Runyon short stories began to dwindle. The majority and the best of his stories were written in the five years from 1931 to 1936. His fiction writing after that time was sporadic. "That period has ended," he remarked, "and the stories are dated."

But Runyon's work continued to be popular for years. Pocket Books, Inc., published a twenty-five-cent copy of *The Best of Damon Runyon,* which sold over a million copies. The same firm brought out a paper-bound edition of *Damon Runyon Favorites,* and again the sales went well over the million mark. Nine hundred thousand copies of this volume were sold. Since there was a demand for Runyon stories, the magazines produced a large crop of imitators. Damon was mystified by the fact that none of the pretenders to his throne were successful. "I don't know why," he said. "I use a very simple formula. I make 'em laugh and I make 'em cry."

8

CIDER IN HIS EAR

"Get the money." There was a period when Runyon said this was the basic, all-prevailing philosophy of his life and outlined a credo for those who cared to espouse a faith in monetary things.

"My measure of success is money," he said.

"I have no interest in artistic triumphs that are financial losers.

"I would like to have an artistic success that also made money, of course, but if I had to make a choice between the two I would take the dough.

"I have learned that when you carry your money to the bank the teller does not hesitate before accepting it to inquire:

" 'Brother, was the enterprise from which this money came of artistic merit or just a commercial winner?'

"Oh, sure, I know this is a sordid attitude. I will abandon it as soon as the world arranges a system of compensation in luxury for an artistic failure equal to that which derives from a commercial success."

Runyon agreed with the old adage—Money isn't everything—which clergymen value so highly as a placating agent for the poor. "It is only 99 per cent of everything," he remarked. Damon advised the youth of the land that if they found it impossible to get rich, they were to get as close to being rich as they could. Other tenets of his monetary religion were: Calamities seldom befall the rich, or at least not in the same proportion that they do the poor or the worse-than-the-poor, the in-betweens, Mr. and Mrs. Mugg; the rich do not stand in line, and the rich do not serve in the ranks.

"It is my observation that the rich have all the best of it in this nation," Damon pontificated when wearing the robes of mammon's chief priest, "and my studies of American History fail to disclose any time when this same situation did not prevail. . . . I know the good book states that 'Love of money is the root of all evil,' but it also says 'Money is a defence,' and that is what I am talking about, money as a defence—a defence in youth against that irksome love in an attic or a housing project, in middle age against the petty laws and regulations that annoy Mr. and Mrs. Mugg, and in old age against fear and disrespect."

Damon got the money. But it also got away from him.

His philosophy neglected the well-founded truism that the more money a person accrues the more he needs. His bankbook fluctuated like the moods of an uncertain woman. Sometimes his bank account would vanish, and the only material proof of his success would be his wardrobe of fifty-dollar shoes, new shirts, monogrammed ties, and a collection of useless doodads. Where did Runyon's money go? He was not a careless spendthrift, but he liked to gamble. He'd bet on anything. He bet on horse races, prize fights, ball games, and card games; he accepted the odds on all and every kind of game, contest of skill or chance. He bet all his life. When he was a boy back in Pueblo he bet the members of his gang that he could pop his toy gun loud enough to make a team of horses run wild. He won the bet. He bet that he could walk into the Stork Club in his shirt sleeves, and he won. He bet that he would revisit the earth after his death.

Some of his friends have said that since he was able to sneak by the headwaiter in the Stork Club while in his shirt sleeves, he should certainly be able to slip through eternity and return from the dead. In Miami he bet on the roller-skating contests; in Saratoga he gambled on the horses. One time he had to take refuge in the United States Hotel in Saratoga when he was unable to cover a bet he had placed on a "sure thing" that also ran. For three days he hid from a bookmaker named "Gloomy Gus." The siege was finally lifted when one of the distress telegrams Damon had sent to friends calling for emergency funds was answered.

In Damon's mind a bet was a bet, a contest a contest. Neither the nature of the contest, nor the location where it

was being held was of any concern to him. He would leave
the comfort and luxury of a mid-town night club to travel
to a water-front dive when he learned of an impending
"ratting" contest.

In a ratting contest young tenement boys would capture
about a dozen hungry rats from the neighborhood pier
sheds and warehouses. The water-front rats, which were
notoriously large and vicious, would be pitted against a
small mongrel with a reputation for tenacity and courage.
Whether it was a ratting contest, or a championship prize
fight, Damon laid his bets with the same intense conviction.

He knew that in his gambling he was emulating the fool
who expected to find a shorter route to heaven. In his
poems and in his columns, he frequently warned his
readers that betting, especially on horses, was the most
expensive of all follies. "The sucker is a terrible institution,"
he said. He knew that the dice came seven only when
you are rolling to make a ten; that a horse never runs
when he is carrying your money.

One of Damon's favorite stories concerned the deathbed
advice a gambler gave his son. One version of the story,
as Damon told it, had his old man delivering the ad-
monition to him when he was graduated from the third
grade.

"Son," the old man said, "as you go around and about
this world, some day you will come upon a man who will
lay down in front of you a new deck of cards with the seal
unbroken and offer to bet he can make the jack of spades
jump out of the deck and squirt cider in your ear.

"Son," the old man said, "do not bet that man, because

just as sure as you do you're going to get an earful of cider."

But Damon's betting was like the drinking of a chronic alcoholic; he could not stop, no matter how badly his vice hurt him. The financial distress he suffered because of gambling never cured him; he could always earn more money. Damon knew what it meant to get his earful of cider.

His poem, "The Gambler's Requiem," which first appeared in the *New York Journal American*, might have been used as his own epitaph. One verse read:

> Lay me away without much noise
>   (Gently, gently, without much noise).
> Lay me away with kindly care,
> And maybe a bit of a prayer.
> Lay me away where I won't hear
>   The roar and the race track news—
> Write me an epitaph big and clear:
>   "Sometimes win, and sometimes lose!"
>   *What does that doctor say of me now?*
>   *Five to one he's wrong!*

One of Damon's most expensive luxuries was the sport of boxing. It was not his unfortunate habit of placing his bets on the contender with the glass jaw that proved so costly, but his insistence on investing his money in the fighters themselves that broke Runyon's bank. Damon realized that his habit of buying "pieces" of fighters was not good business. Even the politicians were more careful with the taxpayers' money than he was with his own earnings. He often said that his interest in prize fighters was one of the basic causes of his writing short stories. Expensive though it was, he followed a dream that he would one day own a heavyweight champion of the world. This ideal fighter would be able to engage Jack Johnson, Jim Corbett, and Jack Dempsey, all in their prime, and Joe Louis, with one hand, while tying his shoelace with his other, meanwhile discussing the merits of blank verse as employed by Shakespeare with Gene Tunney who would be standing in a neutral corner. But the merit of Damon's fighters was in their ability to eat, and sleep, frequently accomplishing the latter on the canvas floor of the ring.

When he was buying a share of stock in a prize fighter, Damon preferred heavyweights to the lighter, more predictable species of boxer. The initial investment was usually the same for any brand of fighter, but the heavyweights were better box-office attractions. The backer of the successful heavyweight was well rewarded for his early confidence in the boy's ability. One of Runyon's great hopes was a 200-pound fighter who seemed to hold extraordinary promise in both fists. Damon was wrong. "He ate himself into the 275-pound class," he explained.

But Damon never gave up hope that some day he would own the heavyweight champion of the world. He sent "Good Time Charley" Friedman to Europe on a one-man argosy to find a potential heavyweight. Good Time Charley returned with an Italian boy named Primo Carnera. But somehow Damon lost out in the maneuvering for financial control of the big Italian. On June 29, 1933, when Carnera won the heavyweight title by knocking out Jack Sharkey in the sixth round, Damon did not own even a minor "piece" of the new champion. His great opportunity had been lost. Damon's chagrin at this defeat was so deep that he immediately sent an emissary to China to investigate a report he had received on the Broadway grapevine that a young Asiatic was cutting fancy didoes in the Chinese ring. Whatever else the scout found in China, he did not locate the pig-tailed pug Damon planned to build into a formidable contender.

Among the heavyweights Runyon sponsored were Wyoming Warner, Napoleon Dorval, and Sailor Hoffman. None of them made ring history. Damon remembered, with some embarrassment, a match he was able to arrange between Sailor Hoffman and Jack Sharkey. During the fight a spectator, disgusted with the ambling antics of the fighters in the ring, yelled out, "Put out the lights, they want to be alone."

Damon was associated for a time with Ed Frayne and Bill Farnsworth, two other Hearst sports writers, in promoting the Milk Fund fights which were sponsored by Mrs. William Randolph Hearst. During this series of boxing matches Mike Jacobs, the Broadway ticket broker, began the career that made him king of the boxing promoters. Since his betting on fights, reporting fights, and ownership of fighters had so deeply enmeshed him in the boxing business, Damon decided to try his hand at promoting fights, too. He collaborated with Rickard, Jimmie Johnston, and Jacobs in promoting prize fights, and was largely responsible for the negotiations that led to the Joe Louis-Max Baer bout in September 1935.

Arranging this fight was no small chore. Ancil Hoffman, Baer's manager, was understandably reluctant to match his fighter against Louis. It was Damon's task to break down his resistance to the match. He finally found an opportunity to use elementary diplomacy on Hoffman. During one of their many conferences, Damon noticed that Hoffman was making frequent trips to the water cooler to apply a tooth-ache powder to a molar that was causing him considerable discomfort. Damon began to talk; he argued, he cajoled, he gossiped, he told stories, and he philosophized. At regular intervals, he paused to remark, "Ancil, you've got to sign up." Whenever the fight was discussed Hoffman said no. Damon continued. He talked for eight hours. By this time Hoffman's face was contorted with pain; all his senses were alive to the agony of his ailing tooth, and it was obvious that only a dentist could relieve him. Hoffman finally surrendered. He agreed to Runyon's terms for the fight. After Hoffman had signed the contracts, Damon handed him a card with the name and address of a dentist printed on it. "Just tell him I sent you," he called after Hoffman, who was hurrying out the door.

The boys were gathered in Lindy's one night when Damon made the statement that he would rather own a great horse than anything else in the world. This caused some surprise among the boys, who could not make it square with Runyon's propensity for acquiring fighters in the hope that one would win the heavyweight throne.

"Would you rather own Seabiscuit than Joe Louis?" one friend asked.

Damon nodded. "You don't have to split the purse with a horse," he said.

Damon knew the horse he wanted, too. He would be a combination of all the best qualities of Seabiscuit, Man o' War, and Whirlaway, and if that horse was not born yet, Damon wanted at least to own a "piece" of his sire or dam. This was not idle Runyon talk. He not only came to own an interest in several racing horses, but at one time he ran a stable of his own and raced his horseflesh property on tracks throughout the East. At this time, Damon shared confidential racing information with his friend Isadore Bieber, another race-horse owner.

Hirsh Jacobs, the noted trainer, helped condition Runyon's horses, among them Tight Shoes, Scribe, Angelic, Euclid. Some of them ran in the money, but they hardly resembled Seabiscuit.

He knew better. His writings furnish unimpeachable testimony to the fact that you cannot beat the horses. In fact he wrote both a poem and a short story titled "All Horse Players Die Broke." If Damon had had his way, the poem would have been distributed to all customers as they entered the gate leading to a race track. Then none of the patrons could plead ignorance of the fact that the averages were working against them when they went broke. He reprinted the poem in his column. He said he wanted each new generation of horse players, who might not have read his verse, to have full knowledge of their inevitable fate:

"ALL HORSE PLAYERS DIE BROKE."

I.

For forty years he's follered the track
And played them horses to hellenback
And there isn't a thing
That he doesn't know—that bloke,
So I sez to him: "I want advice

On beating this dodge at a decent price,
And what do you think you've got to say
To a guy like me, Ol' Soak?"
 Sez he: "Well, son, I've bet and won
 And I've bet and lost and when all is done
 I'm sure of one thing and only one—
 All horse players die broke!

II.

Sez I: "But I see a-many a chump
With plenty of sugar around this dump—"
Sez I: "What system do they employ
Or what is the brand they smoke?"—
Sez I: "You're always doping the dope
And you're doing all right, or so I hope."
Sez I: "I want you to give me a tip
On how I can fill my poke."
 Sez he: "Well, son, this racket's tough
 And I try to learn as I do my stuff,
 And I haven't learned much
 But I've learned enough—
 All horse players die broke!"

III.

Sez he: "Some live to be very old,
'Til their hair turns gray and their blood runs cold,
And some of them almost fall apart
Before they up and croak."
Sez he: "I've seen them, these noble men,
High in the dough and out again,
In fact, I've been there a-many a time myse'f
And that's no joke."

Sez he: "I've seen 'em in limousines
With rocks on their dukes
And dough in their jeans
But they're all alike when they quit these scenes—
All horse players die broke!"

But Damon never learned. In the 1935 Kentucky Derby his pockets were cleaned of everything but his keys and handkerchief when he bet on a horse owned by the late Edward Riley Bradley, who was a personal friend of Damon's. Only a man who had played the horses for years as though it were a part of his religious faith could have written "Monologue of a Horse Player." Only a man like Damon Runyon who knew the bitterness of never retrieving the money lost at the track could have written:

"What did I ever do to anybody?

"Why can't I win?

"Seconds, seconds, seconds.

"All meeting long, seconds, seconds, seconds.

"What did I ever do to anybody?

"I try to live right. I never stole nothing. Why can't I win?

"I bet on favorites and long shots win, and I bet on long shots and favorites win. All the time I get caught in the switches. I got four photo finishes last week. I went down and looked at the pictures and I don't see how the judges could split them out, they were so close. They could have called them either way. I don't know about that camera. It could be wrong. Those judges could be wrong too. I never got a photo finish in my life.

"What did I ever do to anybody?

"I never killed no one. I send money home when I can. I try to treat everybody right.

"Why can't I win?

"How long can a thing like this go on? Can a man come out to the track every day and bet on nearly every race and never get nothing? I wonder if somebody put a curse on me?

"Only winner I had in three weeks was a ten to one shot and I had a fin on him and I thought I was out of all my trouble that day. What do you think come off? They called it a dead heat with the favorite so I only got about half the money that was coming to me."

Damon believed that public gambling had a proper place in society's orderly scheme of things. Acting as a sort of ambassador-at-large from the realm of gambling, Damon did all in his power to gain legal recognition for the betting business, at least as a necessary evil. He had a paternal interest in gambling houses throughout the country, in Bradley's at Palm Beach, Canfield's at Newport and Saratoga, Brown's at French Lick, Palm Island in Miami, and other establishments in Virginia, and Hot Springs, Arkansas. He declaimed against the late Mayor Fiorello H. La Guardia's ban on card playing in restaurants as part of his campaign to drive "the tinhorn" gamblers out of New York. Damon conducted his own passive resistance program against the La Guardia order. Whenever he was in a restaurant he openly exhibited a deck of cards, making a dramatic show of concealing the cards when a minion of the law appeared. Damon's ideas on gambling were similar to his views on prohibition. He contended that attempts to outlaw gambling only drove it underground into the proprietary hands of the criminals and turned a healthy and natural pastime into stealthy, unsavory business.

One incident in Runyon's life indicated how strong were his feelings on gambling. When he was elected dean of the Friars Club, Damon wrote, "I have just been elected dean of the Friars Club, a position that implies greater dignity than has ever before attached to my name." Yet, in 1946, when the conservative members of the Friars Club decided to limit the stakes of the card games, which were operating full-swing at the time, Damon resigned his membership. He considered the rule childish, and castigated the members for bowing to the puritanical preachings of the reformers.

9

THE INNOCENT BYSTANDER

Runyon was eating breakfast in Ratner's Restaurant one morning before he went home to bed. He wrote out his order and handed it to the waiter. "Half a grapefruit, a big bowl of vegetables and sour cream, a big slab of boiled white fish, a bowl of kasha, an order of blintzes, a big piece of coffee cake, and coffee as fast as you can refill my cup." He meant every word of it. When they talked about prodigious appetites along Broadway they talked about Damon Runyon, the gourmet. His favorite eating establishments were Lindy's, Toots Shor's, Dinty Moore's, Gallagher's, and the Stork Club. But he made frequent sorties into strange restaurants in order to sample the food. If it pleased his taste, he returned often. Again and again he visited a Czechoslovakian restaurant on the upper East Side with Irving Hoffman, and many of his nightcap breakfasts were taken in lower East Side Jewish restaurants with other pals.

Damon and Paul Small, the actor's agent, who had the hearty appetite of a growing boy although he was a well-rounded man, had just finished dinner at Lindy's one night when Damon suggested they wander over to Toots Shor's and look over the clientele. Damon had been in the restaurant only a few minutes when he ordered his second full meal.

"Damon, have you lost your memory?" Small said, alarmed. "We just finished dinner fifteen minutes ago."

"Why no," Damon replied, "you can't go to a friend's restaurant and not order something."

Runyon and Small decided one day to go on a diet. After each took a pledge to arrest his appetite in the future by the power of self-control, they went to Lindy's for supper. Runyon ordered chopped liver, borscht, a meat course with three vegetables, and a soufflé for dessert.

"I'll have the same," Small said.

Runyon had finished his fourth cup of coffee when he remarked, "What do you say, Paul, we go on a diet tomorrow?"

Damon sometimes displayed the fastidiousness of an epicure in his eating habits. At one time he was very particular about boiled eggs and made a strong point of

specifying that they had to be boiled for three minutes and
a half. He could tell to a clock-tick how long the cooks had
boiled his eggs and, if their timing was in error by a few
seconds, either below or beyond the time limit, he would
send them back. One day Damon began to consider the
time-lost economics involved in his exacting demands in
the matter of boiled eggs. Through careful calculation he
estimated that the time he wasted in convincing head
waiters that his eggs were not boiled the prescribed three
and a half minutes, added to the time consumed waiting
for a reboiling, amounted to fifteen years! Thereafter he
ate his eggs scrambled. He was fussier about the quality
of each cup of coffee than most people are about their
gin. He spent hours discussing the merits of various blends
of coffee with the restaurateurs of Broadway.

Damon was so interested in all the details of eating that
he classified people according to the way they approached
their food.

There was the unashamed eater. "Of all the many types
of eaters I have studied and classified," Damon said, "I
think I like the unashamed eater best. He is the one that
tears into his chuck without embarrassment and eats until
the cows come home without offering any apologies or
kicking about anything whatever. He is concerned only
with the business of satisfying the inner man. He eats
what is set before him and eats all of it."

The enthusiastic eater. "I like, too, the enthusiastic eater
who boasts as he eats, saying he never tasted such marvel-
ous meat and vegetables in his whole life though this one
can become monotonous after awhile."

The apologetic eater. "The ladies are the greatest

apologetic eaters. They generally alibi with the matter of poundage. A dame hefting a tine will say coyly:

" 'I have to watch my calories. But I'm on a binge tonight so I will have some of that delicious-looking chicken fricassee.' "

The indifferent eater. "This is the eater who, when the waiter proffers a menu, pushes it aside and says languidly:

" 'Oh, just bring me anything. I'm not particular. Anything at all. . . . What's the rest of them having? Stew? Oh, all right. Just bring me some raw oysters, a porterhouse steak with a few sliced tomatoes, some French fried potatoes and a little stewed corn. Eating doesn't really interest me.' "

Damon considered breakfast at Lindy's, which for Broadway society began about 1 P.M., one of the high points of his day. It was there that many of his friends and best informants would gather—the boxers, bookmakers, actors, agents, ticket brokers, radio people, song writers, orchestra leaders, newspapermen, and cops. One afternoon he sat in a corner booth, watching the passing show. Benny Bennett, who was in the box offices of the old and new Madison Square Garden for thirty years, came in and sat next to him.

"The old dogs are petering out," Bennett said, motioning to his feet. "It was all right when they had one or two shows a week at the Garden. Now they have one every night and they are all sellouts and it's rough on the tootsies."

Harry Bestry came in. Someone remarked that Harry was dressed to kill, every hair of his neat little blond mustache in place. "Harry was always a dressy fellow,"

Damon pointed out. "He has—or had—3,000 Charvet neckties, which is more than Charvet has now, 75 suits of clothes by an expensive tailor, 75 pairs of shoes . . . and hats and shirts and overcoats and sweaters. . . ."

This reminded Damon of the story of a friend who once went to call on Bestry. "My friend said he could scarcely open the door of the Bestry apartment, and when he got inside, he had to walk sideways because of the amount of wearing apparel stashed away on the premises."

Damon leaned over to whisper in Bennett's ear. "There's Lieutenant Jimmy Knott, one of the handy-looking young fellows you see on the cops nowadays." Tommy Aulbach was finishing his coffee at one of the tables. "I used to call Tommy 'The Dancing Cop,'" Damon said, "because he loved to trip the light fantastic years ago. He was a good dancer, too. But, you know, of late years I think he has stopped his terpsichorean activities."

"Good Time Charley" Friedman, Jeff Bernie, brother of the late Ben, and "Chuck" Green, known as the oracle of the big street, came in. Sol Green, the fight manager, was eating smoked salmon for breakfast. "Little Niggie" Lawrence, the price maker, walked over to a table where Billy Conn, who was scheduled to fight Joe Louis for the heavyweight title, was eating. Little Niggie told Conn that last night Runyon had been expressing the opinion that Louis would knock Conn out in the first round. Conn gazed at Runyon appalled. Runyon nodded his head.

"I laid Runyon $2000 to $200 against his notion," Little Niggie said. "Then a guy comes in and says 'Nig, you owe me fifty dollars.' I say, 'For what?' He says 'I win from you on the hockey game!' I say 'You must be nuts. I never bet you on no hockey game.' He says, 'Yes, you did. I guess you forgot it. Sambo was there at the time.' I say, 'If Sambo says I bet you, I will pay.' So he goes out and gets Sambo and Sambo says 'Yes, Nig, you bet him all right.' So I pay and Runyon sits there and sees this come-off.

"Then," Little Niggie continued, "Runyon offs his bets with me and when I ask him why, he says 'I do not bet with anybody who has amnesia.' Who is amnesia?"

Conn continued to stare at Runyon, who again nodded his head confirming Little Niggie's story.

"You can bet me he don't knock me out in fifteen if you like," Conn said.

"I was only kidding, Nig," Damon replied.

Conn was knocked out by Louis!

Runyon always kept his feet well dressed, but it was through his friendship with Phocian Howard, editor of the *New York Press*, a racing paper, that Damon was converted to the religion of sartorial splendor. Phocian maintained a house at Saratoga during the racing season. He said the newspaper boys were always welcome. They did not need a second invitation. Phocian's was more than a home and a city room to them. They ate, slept, drank, and sometimes worked there. Phocian had a Rolls Royce, and hired a chauffeur to drive it. The chauffeur was noted for his loyalty. Even when Howard's fortunes at the track took an unfortunate turn and he had no money to buy gasoline, the chauffeur stood by. When Phocian appeared at the track, people turned away from where the thoroughbreds were running to watch a well-dressed man go by.

Like most converts, Damon outdid his master in his

adulation of the wardrobe. As part of the ritual in honor
of the new fetish, Damon made a complete change of
clothes every four hours. "It renews my spirit," he explained.

Dave Levy, vice-president of Nat Lewis' Broadway
clothes shop, was one of the high priests of haberdashery
who counseled Damon on his clothes.

Dave and Damon first met in about 1916.

"No doubt you know what I do," Damon said, clasping
Dave's hand. "What's your racket?"

Dave said he was employed by Nat Lewis, the haber-
dasher.

"When can I come in to see you to buy some nooses?"
Damon asked.

"Nooses?"

"Certainly, nooses. That means cravats. You're a Nat
Lewis man, you know what cravat means, don't you?"

Damon began buying his cravats at Nat Lewis', and
he and Dave became close friends. Damon made the shop
one of his headquarters, where he met his friends and
Broadway acquaintances, listened to their gossip, their
troubles, and their schemes for quick happiness and easy
money. After reading Damon's column, which reported the
conversations in the haberdashery, Dave suspected him
of maintaining a membership in the psychic world. All
the idle talk had been recorded word for word, yet Damon
had never taken a note while he was in the store.

Nat Lewis' old store was on Broadway between Forty-
seventh and Forty-eighth Streets under the Palais D'Or,
where Paul Whiteman became famous. The store ran from
Broadway through to Seventh Avenue. It was Damon's

practice to begin his daily shopping trip at the shirt counter near the Broadway entrance, and buy his way from counter to counter until he reached the robe cases at the Seventh Avenue side of the store. He bought more robes than he had space for in his closet. He collected sweaters the way some people collect postage stamps. One season a supposedly distinctive new sweater was enjoying a brief fad along Broadway. Damon took one look. He went home and brought out an old sweater he had bought twenty years before. It was an exact reproduction of the new style. "I was always twenty years ahead of the times," Damon boasted.

He was a man of many hats. He bought narrow-brim hats, and wide-brim hats, and hats of many materials, from felt to beaver. When a friend admired his hat, Damon took it off his head and gave it to him as a present. When a hat style captured Damon's fancy he would buy a large assortment of them. Then, as he learned the head sizes of his cronies, he would distribute them along Broadway.

He bought canes, but he never carried them. One day he bought eight Malacca canes with ram's-horn handles ranging in price from $50 to $200 each.

He bought extra-large-sized linen handkerchiefs and had his full name hand-embroidered in script on the two-inch hem.

Long before the public became aware of harmony in clothes' combinations, Nat Lewis and Damon created brocaded silk shirts, undershirts, shorts, and pajamas in matching designs and colors. They cost $150 a set.

When Damon had trouble with his laundry service he and Nat Lewis made up a seven-day Navy blue shirt.

Each day he bought a supply of English and French hose.

"Is there anything new?" Damon asked on one of his routine visits to the Nat Lewis store.

"New!" Nat said. "We have some new ties, new socks, new shirts, new sweaters, new robes, new canes and—"

Damon raised his hand. "Halt. I want a new story." Dave, who had been listening, asked Damon if he had ever heard of "klab."

"What's that, a dish? What kind of a dish is that?"

Dave explained that klab was the abbreviated name for a Hungarian card game named klabiash. Damon had never heard of the game, but he insisted that he would learn to play that day. Dave and Damon left the store and went to the Runyon apartment in the Hotel Forrest. All that day the two men played klab. The next day Damon wrote an enthusiastic story about it in his column. His readers responded immediately; their letters dissented, argued, and called for more details. For two weeks Damon devoted his column to klab; rules were defined, anecdotes related, and the finer points of the game discussed.

For a time Runyon made an intense study of klab, and then announced his verdict of the world's champion player. He was John Popkin, owner of the Hickory House, a restaurant on West Fifty-second Street. "John Popkin is the outstanding klabiash player of the decade," Damon reported in his column. "His prowess is known all over the country."

When Jack Dempsey came to town to fight John Lester Johnson in Dempsey's first appearance at the Harlem Sporting Club, Damon introduced him to Nat Lewis. Later, when Dempsey became the heavyweight champion and was training for the Firpo fight, Nat showed Damon a shaker knit sweater he was giving to the fighter. Runyon suggested that Dempsey's name be lettered on the back of the sweater. Nat thought that might be a nice touch, carried it out, and a new fad was born.

"Meet Rudolph Valentino, " Nat Lewis said one day when Damon was ambling through the store on his daily inspection tour. The movie idol was shopping for a dressing gown, and Nat was displaying some fine brocaded silks from Paris and Switzerland.

Runyon suggested that Nat create something entirely new for Rudolph.

"But what?" Nat asked.

"Yes, what?" Valentino echoed.

"A robe made of leopard skins," Damon replied.

Valentino was delighted with the idea, so Nat made him a leopard-skin robe.

About a year later, Damon received a package from Valentino. He had sent the leopard robe to Runyon as a gift. He called up Dave Levy and told him the news. "I'm going to go him one better," Runyon said. "Davy—get me a set of leopard skins and make me a pair of slippers to match this robe."

Although he bought more expensive clothes than he could ever hope to wear, Damon loved a bargain. One particularly bad winter in New York, when the streets remained a morass of gray slush for months, Runyon became annoyed with the inadequacy of his ordinary rubber shoes. He went on a shopping expedition for a pair of old-fashioned, four-buckle arctics. He found them in Gimbel's basement and was delighted with the discovery.

Damon was once named as one of the ten best-dressed men. On this occasion Broadway observed that when Runyon concentrated on perfecting either a talent or a habit he usually produced startling results. After he received this sartorial honor Runyon found amusement composing his own "great" lists. His unofficial lists included great eaters, great songs, great fighters, great dressers, great haters, and great singers. Damon worked out elaborate handicaps for each contender.

Following the success of his short stories, Runyon was able to afford his luxurious taste for expensive shoes. He only wished he might be spared the agony of breaking them in. One night he was sitting in a restaurant with the late Hype Igoe, the sports writer, and T. A. Dorgan, better known as Tad, the cartoonist.

"I bought a new pair of shoes today," Damon remarked, "I only wish there were some way I could have them broken in for me."

"Why don't you get someone to warm them up?" Tad suggested.

Igoe did not offer any advice.

"By the way, Hype," Tad said, "what size do you wear?"

"All right," Igoe said, "you'd find out anyway. I wear 5½B." This was Runyon's size. From then on Hype was spared the expense of buying shoes. When he had broken in one pair, Runyon bought him another.

On July 8, 1932, Damon married Patrice Amiti del Grande, twenty-five-year-old native of Spain, at the home of Mr. and Mrs. Ed. Frayne, 200 West Sixteenth Street. Damon's old friend, Mayor James J. Walker, officiated at the ceremony. Patrice, who was known professionally as

Patrice Gidier, had been a member of Texas Guinan's troupe. She had met Damon through Harry Richman at the Club Richman. Damon first took his bride to live in his three-room penthouse apartment in the Hotel Forrest, but they later moved to the Parc Vendome, a more pretentious establishment.

Being married did little to alter Runyon's living habits. His day began at 1 p.m., when he would arise and eat breakfast. His breakfast menu was always the same: a bowl of fruit, boiled kidneys, toast, and several cups of coffee. Then he would go over to Broadway for a stroll. He chatted with the neighbors of Fifty-second Street, visited Nat Lewis' shop, and paid calls on the other clothing and jewelry stores he patronized. He only returned home to change his clothes. Patrice and Damon usually ate dinner with one, or several, of his cronies. After dinner they would go to a movie, sometimes two in a single evening. Their quality didn't interest him; he just liked movies. Patrice usually stayed by Damon's side until 2 a.m. while he took up his research into the city's nocturnal life. Then she went home to bed. Damon remained at Lindy's or the Stork Club drinking coffee until dawn. Arriving home, he read the late evening and early morning papers, and then went to his typewriter and wrote his column before he went to bed.

"Mr. Runyon, why do you spend so much time in restaurants and night clubs?" a curious sightseer asked him.

"I've been breathing the air of jernts of all kinds all my life and prefer it to the open air," Damon replied.

Damon was certainly loquacious, but he was also one

of the best listeners of his time. He would sit at his table for hours lending his ear to underworld characters, chorus girls, bookmakers, cops, freaks, waiters, columnists, boxers, fellow newspapermen, jockeys, and to almost anyone who came along. "I will stay up later than any living man, but have trouble finding people to stay up with me. I love to gab. I have a sour pan and a merry heart."

But Runyon did not always have a merry heart, and his moods were utterly unpredictable. One day he would be talkative, charming, and pleasing to everyone who greeted him. The following night he would be silent and oppressive. When he was depressed he hurt many people by not recognizing them. On the other hand, he thought nothing of presenting his most expensive and treasured clothes to some pal. At times he changed his mind on an important subject with every sip of coffee, and then he would remain adamant on some trivial matter to the point of being ridiculous. He despised ostentation, but he bragged about his expensive ties.

Although he glorified Broadway in his columns and short stories, and considered this part of New York to be his best friend, he often repeated his remark, "If you have two friends on Broadway consider yourself a success."

No one knew Runyon intimately; he was a true enigma, perhaps even to himself.

Runyon's periods of silence were never explained. They were just there, unannounced, and his friends understood their presence. He once traveled from New York to New Orleans with the late Bill McGeehan, sports editor and columnist for the *New York Herald Tribune*, without speaking a word.

When the train was moving into New Orleans station, McGeehan commented, "Nice trip."

Runyon considered this a moment. "Okay," he said.

Ring Lardner, the short-story writer, had similar spells of silence. Two weeks before Lardner died, in September 1933, Damon visited him in the hospital.

"Hello, Damon," Lardner greeted him as he entered the room.

"Hello, Ring," Runyon said, taking a seat on the edge of Lardner's bed. Neither man spoke for half an hour. Lardner broke the silence.

"Who was the greatest pitcher in the world?" he asked.

"Matty," Runyon replied. He meant Christy Mathewson, one of baseball's great pitchers, who had played with the New York Giants.

Lardner, who preferred Walter Johnson, of the Washington Senators, rolled over on his side.

"Goodbye," he said.

"Goodbye," Runyon replied, and left.

Runyon sometimes devised ludicrous explanations to cloak his personal feuds.

Leonard Lyons, a columnist for the *New York Post,* once saw him turn his back on a man everyone considered to be an old friend. The two were inseparable during the days Runyon wrote a sports column for the *New York American.*

"Are you angry with him?" Lyons asked.

"He was arrested in an arson case when his factory burned down," Runyon replied.

"Is that why you're angry with him?"

"Well," Runyon said, "I always resented their finding the *New York American*'s sport section soaked in oil."

Runyon was willing to listen to most anyone, except bores. He once passed an entire night at the Stork Club maneuvering to avoid one.

"What's the matter?" a friend asked. "Have you stopped talking to him?"

"No," Runyon said. "Listening to him."

One night a perennial pest cornered Damon at a table at Toots Shor's. Runyon noticed Jack O'Brian, the Associated Press drama critic, sitting near by, and was able to pass him a note. "I wanna duck this guy," the note read. Jack promptly went to Damon's relief. He walked over to the table, and began regaling Runyon about a wonderful show that had just opened at a downtown night club. Damon jumped to his feet.

"I must get down and see that show right away," he said, with sham excitement. "There might be a story in it."

Damon was not only released from the bore, but he visited the night club and thoroughly enjoyed himself.

Some newspapermen did not escape the circle of people Damon regarded with caustic antipathy. When one of these reporters or columnists passed his table in a restaurant or night club, Damon would nod in recognition, and then scribble a few words on a slip of paper. The verdict frequently read, "Big heel." Yet it was also part of Runyon's nature to encourage and help the cub reporter.

During the Winter Olympics at Lake Placid in 1932 a young reporter for one of the news services was awakened from his sleep one night by a phone call from his chief. "Is this assignment too big for you?" the editor asked. The reporter paced the floor all night. He had put all his effort into his work, and yet he was being rebuked. The next morning he confessed his failure to Lewis Burton, of the

New York Journal American. Burton commiserated with the hapless reporter and told him not to worry. At lunch that day Burton mentioned the incident to Runyon.

"I tell you what you do," Runyon said. "Bring the guy over to see me this afternoon. Make it casual. Say to him, 'Let's drop over and say hello to Runyon,' or something like that. Don't let him know it's framed."

Later in the day Burton and the discouraged reporter dropped in on Runyon.

"I've been wanting to meet you," Damon said. "You know, I think the stuff you've been filing is the best that has come out of here."

The reporter was too excited to blush, or even offer a modest thank you. "You do?" he said. "But I just got a terrific calling down from my boss. He claims I'm throwing too much extra stuff in."

Damon shook his head and laughed. "That old geezer, don't pay any attention to him. He's probably got stomach trouble. Most editors have. Just keep on writing. It's good."

By a simple ruse, Damon had been able to restore the young man's confidence, and in the clear light of his new faith, the reporter saw the faults in his stories.

Nick Kenny, who is now radio columnist for the *New York Daily Mirror,* was introduced to Runyon at a baseball writers' party during the 1924 World Series. Kenny was then the sports editor of a New Jersey paper.

"Nick Kenny?" Damon said. "I know that name. Do you write poetry?"

Kenny admitted rather sheepishly that he had been sending poems to Arthur Brisbane.

"He's been sending them on to me," Damon said, amused

at the coincidence. "Wants me to tell him if it's real poetry.
I've got a drawer full of your stuff."

"Tell him it has something, will you?" Kenny pleaded.
"I want to get into the big time."

"Okay, kid," Runyon said, "I'll tell him."

A week later Kenny was working for one of Hearst's
newspapers—the *Boston American.*

In one of his columns, Dan Parker, sports editor of the
New York Mirror, also attested to this quality in
Damon:

"Many writers owe a great deal to Damon Runyon's un-
solicited help. Speaking only for myself, I couldn't begin to
enumerate the kind deeds Damon has done for me, dating
back twenty years when I arrived in New York with the
hayseed falling out of my pockets and very much awed by
the big city. It was Damon who first taught me that really
big men don't try to impress others with their importance.
I was sitting next to him at a World Series game, feeling as
if I were in the presence of royalty—as indeed I was—and,
with one friendly, unassuming remark, Damon brought
himself down to my level and put me completely at
ease."

Bradley Kelly of King Features recalls that his late boss
Joe Connolly had standing orders from William Randolph
Hearst to get a Runyon story every week. Damon had
slackened his pace lately and, according to Kelly, "Damon
said it was Connolly's and my Irish blarney that squeezed
those stories out of him. Damon would sit across the desk
and holler like a stuck pig, but we had to get those
stories."

Kelly was also reminded of the time newspaper colleagues gave a Banshee luncheon in honor of Damon Runyon. The master of ceremonies asked Damon for his favorite newspaper story. Here it is:

"Bugs Baer was writing on the *Evening World* under his own name and on another paper under an assumed one. Hearst wired New York, 'I think Graham is writing better stuff than Baer. . . . Get him!'" Graham was, of course, Baer's pen name on the other paper.

There was no doubt that Damon loved Manhattan, although he insisted that it was proof that a man had incipient insanity if he lived there when he had any other place to go. Perhaps Damon did grow weary of New York at times, for he created another place where he could go. He built a $75,000 villa on Hibiscus Island, off Miami Beach in Florida.

Both Damon and Patrice enjoyed Florida. He, in particular, liked the warm sand under his feet, the privacy of his own estate, and although he couldn't distinguish a wren from a flamingo, or identify the flowers on his estate, he admitted that the tropical nature in Florida afforded a lesson in physical contentment that should be a required experience for every soul. Besides, he was near Hialeah race track in Miami. One of Damon's neighbors on Hibiscus Island was "Big Frenchy" Demange, alias George Fox, a former racketeer king who had retired into a life of relative tranquility. Fox owned a number of Great Danes who harbored the idea that it was their duty to keep Runyon in good physical shape by giving him a daily workout. When the giant dogs saw Damon walking home they formed a pack and galloped toward him. When he saw them moving in his direction, he sprinted to the nearest palm tree. By maintaining a firm embrace on the tree, he was able to withstand their first assault. The dogs treated Damon as a friend, but he never reciprocated their affection.

Damon had become a gin rummy enthusiast. He first saw Louis Sobol, the columnist, and Dr. Leo Michel, the court physician to the potentates of Broadway, playing the game in 1940. The fact that you could carry on a conversation while playing the game intrigued Damon, and he soon adjudged himself the nation's leading master and oracle of gin rummy play. Certainly, his manners when he lost were fitting for a despot. He hated to lose. One evening while playing gin with Ken Kling, the race horse analyst, Damon had an extended run of bad luck. He lost his temper and picked up the deck of cards and winged them at Kling.

Runyon was frequently questioned about his quaint habits. It was only natural that people would want to know why he spent so much of his time playing gin rummy.

"A monkey can play it as well as a man," one friend observed.

"Your theory is all wrong," Damon said. "A monkey plays it far better."

While at Hibiscus Island he hired Eddie "The Horsethief" Burke as a chauffeur. Eddie was not engaged because he was a fast and careful driver, but because he played the type of gin that suited Damon's temperament. Every time Damon threatened to fire him, Eddie knew he had been winning too many games from his boss.

In August 1941, Damon signed a contract as a writer-producer for RKO pictures. The boys in Lindy's were properly astounded by this development in Runyon's career. Would Runyon separate himself from New York by a distance of 3000 miles? Broadway amused itself by speculating on this question. Certainly, Runyon did not have to leave New York to make money in Hollywood, they argued; he merely had to write a short story, and in due time Hollywood would make it into a movie.

The first Runyon story to be adapted for the screen was "Madame La Gimp," which became *Lady for a Day* when it was produced in 1933, starring May Robeson. The movie was a success with both the critics and the audience. It received three Academy Award prizes; one went to the director, a second to the adapters, and the third to the star.

Hollywood then made *Little Miss Marker*, with Shirley Temple playing the little girl whose charm converted the criminals and gamblers of Runyon's story into sentimental, soft-hearted gentlemen. Runyon stories came from Hollywood as movies in a steady flow: *"Lemon Drop Kid," Midnight Alibi*, from the story, "The Old Doll's House," *Million Dollar Ransom, Three Wise Guys, Princess O'Hara, Tight Shoes, A Slight Case of Murder*, from the Runyon-Lindsay play.

"Runyon only has to say that 'Oh' and a film company will buy it," one Hollywood agent remarked.

Damon had his own version of why Hollywood offered him a job. According to him, several producers, directors, writers, and assorted executives were called to an emergency conference.

"We must get someone to write the dialogue for those

Damon Runyon characters in the next movie," the chief executive explained. "Everybody think hard now."

There were several suggestions, but none was acceptable.

Finally, a minor vice president, who had not spoken since the conference began, said, "Boss, why don't we get Damon Runyon?"

"Why yes," the executive said, "as a last resort that seems like a good idea."

Whatever the motives that prompted the movie executives to invite Runyon to Hollywood, it seemed to be an intelligent experiment. Runyon was not only a writer, but a movie fan, who knew the tastes of the audience. Late in 1941 Damon and Patrice were safely ensconced in their own home in Beverly Hills. Damon had difficulty acclimating himself to his new environment. In fact, for the first two weeks he not only expressed abhorrence of Hollywood, but openly loathed the entire state of California.

Leo Spitz and his wife, Frankie James, helped Damon become fond of Hollywood, despite the fact that he still harbored certain objections that time or experience could never wipe out. Damon said he had "a mole's dislike of sunshine and fresh air." In Hollywood he was subjected to both sunshine and fresh air, but he did his best to combat their insidious influence. The shades in his home and office were always drawn against the day. Even during the summer he appeared in an ankle-length suede coat, and grumbled at every intrusive breeze. The necessity for rising early was the real cross he had to bear, for though Mike Lyman's and Prince Mike Romanoff's restaurants served the Hollywood counterparts of Lindy's and the

Stork Club, he could never keep, in Hollywood, the hours he kept on Broadway. And, though he boasted that no one had ever paid a check while he was at the table, he never got used to paying the telegraph toll charges on his syndicated column. Lou Irwin and Bob Goldstein were constant pals to Damon in those days.

After five months with RKO, Damon signed a contract to write and produce pictures for 20th Century-Fox films. He was a good producer. He worked hard, kept within his budget, and left the technical details of movie making to the men who understood them. He tried to analyze each scene as though he were seeing it through the eyes of the average audience, and he was particularly adept at this, because he, himself, personified the average audience. Before the cameras had recorded a single scene of one of Runyon's productions, *The Big Street,* he and Irving Reis, who was to direct the movie, flew to Manhattan. Damon escorted Reis along Broadway introducing him to his entire cast of characters. Several hours later Damon turned to his director. "Good night, Irving," he said. "I think you can direct the picture now."

Before *The Big Street* was released, Damon saw it over a hundred times. The sentimental scenes never failed to affect him, but he tried to camouflage his feelings by coughing and pretending to be seeking some mislaid object on the floor. He was present the day the film was previewed by the "Deathwatch" (the name given to the sound, camera, and musical technicians, who never comment on the worth of any film). After it was over, he turned to Reis. "Gee, Irving," he said, "it didn't play so good today, did it?"

When *The Big Street* was released in September 1942, it received good reviews. The film critics, however, seemed just as bewildered by the unorthodox plot and unusual display of characters in this Runyon movie as the theater critics had been by the stage play, *A Slight Case of Murder*. *Time* magazine said: "*The Big Street* is a pleasant bit of paranoia that cannot possibly displease anyone but may baffle some cinemaddicts for a while."

When Runyon adapted and produced *Butch Minds the Baby,* he decided to add a few words to the highly stylized vocabulary that had become known as Runyonese. He invented the word "mooley" to mean a person of small intellect, and the word "Komoppo," which he defined as a lady who flaunts her wealth. A few days after he had submitted the script to the censors, Damon received a notice from the Hays Office demanding his appearance before their board. The censors told him that they were prepared to censor the film because of the unknown words in the script. They demanded that Runyon furnish their derivation, definition, and "of what language they are a part."

"I made them up myself," Runyon said. The script was approved.

In one of the scenes of *Butch Minds the Baby* a young goat was needed. There seemed to be a shortage of goats in the Hollywood area. After some search, Damon was finally able to find one, but only at an exorbitant fee.

"We'll get even with it," Damon said. "When the picture is finished we'll have it roasted and served."

After seeing the first preview of the picture, Damon changed his mind. "That's a cute kid," he remarked. "I guess we'll give it a reprieve." He gave the goat back to its previous owner with instructions that the animal be put out to pasture.

When Runyon returned to Hibiscus Island for a vacation he usually brought company with him. Irving Caesar, the song writer, who characterized Damon as being a supreme cynic saved by a flash of humor, passed two winters with him. During one of their retreats, Damon and Irving wrote a movie script called "Straight, Place, and Show." When the picture was released not a single word, scene or situation the pair had written was used. Irving was upset, and called the movie a disgrace.

"Suppose the movie is a hit, then are you going to squawk?" Damon asked.

The movie was a financial success, with Runyon and Caesar receiving equal billing as the authors of the script. Irving never squawked.

Despite his experiences with George Fox's Great Danes in Florida, Damon loved dogs. "I would not like to be without a dog," he once remarked, and he seldom was. When he lost a dog he took an oath that he would never own another because the experience of loving and losing a favorite was too depressing. "Then as time dulled the edge of my sorrow I have invariably found myself looking around for another dog," he said. "I find myself wandering about peering into the pet shop windows and watching the puppies at play, not at all disheartened by their environment, and wishing I could buy every last one of them and take them home with me."

Damon realized that many people did not fancy dogs, and conceded their right to these views. "Only I wish they might have known little Nubbin when she was well and seen her glad responsiveness to a friendly word or look."

Nubbin was a red cocker spaniel Damon owned while he was in Hollywood. When Nubbin became ill, he took her to Dr. Eugene C. Jones, who owned one of the finest pet hospitals in Southern California. Damon was so impressed with the appointments and sterilized atmosphere that he said he was hoping to sneak a few of his friends in there because accommodations in the regular hospital were very scarce. Dr. Jones said Nubbin had to have her tonsils out. Damon watched the operation, and reported that Dr. Jones did a neat job. He had a lady assistant listening to Nubbin's heart through a stethoscope and warning the doctor now and then to quit pushing the anaesthetic cone tighter.

"Her heart won't stand it," the lady assistant would say.

The tonsillectomy was successful, but Nubbin developed uremic poisoning. Damon visited Nubbin almost every day at the pet hospital. One day he complained that he was having trouble with his own throat. Dr. Jones offered to take a look at it, although, he said, ailing human beings were not quite in his line. Damon accepted the offer. When he finished his examination, Dr. Jones told Damon to go to a throat specialist immediately.

But Damon hesitated; he feared trouble. He recalled the time in 1931 when his tonsils were removed by Dr. Julius Lempert, the ear, nose, and throat specialist. The tonsillectomy had been difficult. Dr. Lempert said he had removed as many as 90,000 tonsils without the slightest kickback until he came to Damon's. Damon had had to spend several weeks in the hospital recovering from the operation, and before he left Dr. Lempert warned him that his throat was not of the ordinary variety and might cause trouble later.

Damon said Dr. Lempert was one of the kindest men he had ever known. And now he came back to New York to see him. It was difficult for a kind man to announce the results of the examination. Damon had cancer. Dr. Lempert sent him to Dr. Jules C. Abels, at the Memorial Hospital, where it was determined that Damon's larynx would have to be removed. Just before the operation in November 1944, a group of friends assembled around his hospital bed. "I've got no kick coming," Damon said. "All over the world today, on every front, youngsters are being shot at. I've lived a full life in sixty odd years. No, I've got no kick coming."

The operation silenced his voice. From then on a pad of notepaper and a pencil were his means of communication.

As soon as he was able to sit up, Damon returned to writing his column. He started by kidding himself.

"Runyon, old boy, you'd better get your nose up against the grindstone again. Put your shoulder to the wheel and your best foot forward or your name is glucose."

He lauded his pal Irving Hoffman "for keeping his hellos up big and strong all the way through." He then told about someone who had mysteriously entered his hospital room; he was a man in "beautifully tailored, soft white flannels."

" 'Oh hello,' I said. . . . 'I was not expecting you. . . . If you will just hand me my katy and my coat I will be with you in a jiffy.'

" 'Tut-tut-tut,' Death said. 'Not so fast, I have not come for you. . . '"

10

DAMON AND PYTHIAS

It was 6:15 A.M. and summer when Walter Winchell drove
his passenger to the entrance of the Buckingham Hotel on
West Fifty-seventh Street. Damon Runyon, now a gaunt,
tired man, opened the door of the car, and backed slowly
out into the morning light. It was the time of day he referred
to as "the tubercular light of the morning." He gripped the
handle of the car door to steady himself and pulled the brim
of his hat over his eyes. As he shuffled toward the entrance
of his home, he turned and waved a weary salute to his

friend. Winchell watched Damon as his hunched form disappeared into the shadows of the hotel lobby. He toyed with his steering wheel, reluctant to drive away. "Poor guy," Winchell muttered, "nothing to go home to but four walls. I hate to leave him alone. He never wants to go home."

In the hotel elevator, Damon braced himself against the brass hand rail. He groped through his pockets fingering for his keys. It had been an exciting night. During the last few hours of darkness a moment in the life of New York had been suspended in time. He and Winchell had come upon the scene while they were prowling through the city on their nightly patrol. When he reached his room, Damon was not even conscious of routine habits. He sat at his typewriter without removing his hat. The poignant features of the night's dramatic incident formed a clean design in his mind. Damon was tired, but sleep might destroy the picture.

He began his column: "The fight between the legless man and the chattering Latin was the most bizarre incident I ever witnessed in all my many years on Broadway. The telling really calls for a Zola, not a Runyon. . . ."

The drama was reaching its climax when Damon and Winchell arrived. They had been driving through the Manhattan streets, listening to the police radio in Winchell's car, keeping a close lookout, seeking adventure—a fire, an alarm calling the police to a homicide, a holdup, an accident. Perhaps they would find out something of the personality of this town—half human, half animal—in some street happening. Their search ended on the short stretch of Fifty-first Street between Broadway and Seventh Avenue. A slender and dark Latin who looked like the

male half of an adagio team sat on a door stoop heckling
a legless man who stared at him from the sidewalk.

The well-dressed Latin was drunk and poured out a
stream of shrill chatter. He spoke in his native tongue,
but the handful of spectators knew his language was
abusive. They understood that he was insulting the legless
man. The legless man who wore a dark short-sleeved sports
shirt, open at the throat, the tail fluttering loosely about
his body, had removed the small platform he used to
transport himself through the streets. He waited on the
sidewalk, a cigar stub between his lips, a joyless smile on
his mouth. Suddenly the Latin came down from the steps
and kicked the legless man in the stomach; then, with one
agile movement, the legless man grabbed the Latin around
the knees and brought him to the sidewalk. Damon and
Winchell stood near by watching.

"They rolled over and over out into the filthy gutter,"
Runyon wrote, "the Latin uppermost and his voice now
rising to a shriek as he shouted epithets, the legless man
silent but his hands and arms busy like the slowly en-
veloping folds of a python about its prey as he gradually
worked his body on top of the Latin and his right arm
across the Latin's throat.

" 'Now you're going to sleep,' he said to the chattering
Latin, apparently applying pressure, though not, I am
sure, as much as he could. It is my opinion that he could
have broken the Latin's neck or choked him to death had
he wished, but was only giving him a good scare.

" 'Watch him go to sleep,' he urged the circle of spectators, shirtsleeved, bareheaded, night owls of all kinds, cab
drivers, fight managers, waiters, bookies. They eyed the

tableau silently, impassively. The legless man's garments
began slipping from his body disclosing his white skin and
one sensitive spectator hastily departed. Another bent
down and bawled into the ears of the grapplers that the
cops were coming but this did not end the struggle.

"I think the legless man may have relaxed his muscles
an instant or the Latin was more slippery than he thought
because suddenly the Latin squirmed loose, leaped to his
feet and ran away a few yards, stopped and began shrilling
at the legless man. The latter pulled himself up on the
sidewalk and conferred briefly with a Lilliputian who was
among the spectators, and apparently counseled peace.
The legless man still had the cigar stub in his mouth. The
Latin kept screaming from a distance.

"Suddenly the legless man made a dive for him, moving
in great bounds with incredible speed almost entirely on
his hands. Afterwards a spectator told me he had seen the
legless man run that way for two blocks. The Latin fled.

" 'How you gonna fight a guy who runs like that?' demanded the legless man as he returned to his little wagon,
the cigar stub waggling in his mouth.'"

Damon asked Winchell to drive the legless man home.
The cripple was pleased and unfastened his wagon when
he climbed into the back seat. "I don't want to cut the
cushions of your car," he said. "I was just teaching that
guy not to run over people." Damon turned in his seat to
question him, but before he would answer any questions,
he asked Damon to feel his muscles. Damon fingered the
legless man's arms, wrists, and shoulders; they were solid,
hard, like iron. The man was pleased. He said his name
was James Lambeth and he was forty-two years old and

married. He lost his legs in a bombing raid in World War I when he served with the 69th Regiment of the Rainbow Division.

"Drive me over to West 40th Street off Tenth Avenue there," the legless man instructed. "You'll see it. It's a red-brick house. I live in a four-room apartment on the first floor, in the front. I've got a cat with seven kittens. Watch when I get out; I'll whistle and the cat will come to the window. She always comes to the window when I whistle."

Winchell found the red-brick house and drove up to the curb. The legless man had no trouble getting out of the car. When he was on the sidewalk, he whistled, and in a moment a tabby could be seen peering out the front window.

"I thought it most considerate of the gentleman to want to avoid cutting the cushions," Damon noted as Winchell pointed the car north on Tenth Avenue.

"Look at my hat!" Winchell moaned, holding up his crumpled fedora. "He sat all over my hat!"

Winchell's friendship and his early morning drives with the columnist had become an integral part of Damon's life after the operation that removed his larynx. Up to this time, Winchell and Runyon had not been close friends, although when Runyon began writing short stories Winchell had been near to encourage him, and to still his doubts when Damon's self-confidence was on the ebb.

Now he returned to be a friend and a companion as the shadows of loneliness settled over Damon. At 3 A.M. in the Stork Club, he would leave with any friends who wished to accompany him on a cruise through the streets of Manhattan. When an alarm that seemed exciting came

over the radio, Winchell would speed to the crime or accident, sometimes beating the police car to the scene.
Runyon called the columnist's hobby "little boy stuff" until
Winchell piqued his interest by regaling him with a few
of the stories that he had seen break out of the early hours
of darkness. Runyon decided to join Winchell in a few
experimental rides. Before long the pair were inseparable
partners in the dawn patrol, and their friendship grew.
They became known as Damon and Pythias. Winchell
called Damon "the Master" or "the Brain" and his sympathy and admiration for his older colleague was almost
a devotion. Runyon treated Winchell like a precocious
younger brother; he regarded Walter's perennial enthusiasm with fond tolerance, and tried to tease him into affect-
ing a more dignified manner. But it would be easier to
tame the forces of the atom than to persuade Winchell to
quiet his approach to life. He knew his job, and no one
could change the way he conducted his business.

But Broadway was not ready to understand Runyon's
sudden affection for Winchell. One of the representatives
of the Big Street informed Runyon of the doubts, telling
him that the Runyon-Winchell friendship had become a
leading topic of conversation around town. Damon scribbled a note in reply. "When a guy's got class, I got to go
with him." Early in World War II, Winchell called for in-
tervention by the United States against Hitler, and he
frequently used his column to bludgeon the isolationists
who were attempting to obstruct President Roosevelt's
policies. Winchell in turn was attacked from the floor of
Congress. His critics called him a "Stork Club Admiral."
Runyon defended his friend. The record of Winchell's

Navy career in both world wars appeared in Damon's column; in several articles he offered facts tending to prove that Winchell was not a meddler, but an earnest patriot.

Runyon's life now emanated from Table 50 in the Cub Room of the Stork Club. After his evening movie, Damon usually arrived at the Cub Room at about 11:30. Near midnight the permanent members of the Table 50 coterie— Irving Hoffman, Paul Small, Leonard Lyons, Jimmy Cannon, "Chuck" Green, Eddie Walker, Winchell and Runyon —gathered at the club. Sherman Billingsley acted as the group's general patron and sergeant-at-arms. The waiters called Table 50 the "blasting block," for it was the habit of this group to declare all subjects open to discussion. Opinions were expected to be varied, dissenting, and controversial. Agreement was reached on only one subject— women. Someone said: "It's the man who pays," and this was accepted as a truism. Women, who received a large share of the conversational play, were usually given bad notices. But whenever a lady passed through the Cub Room all conversation at Table 50 stopped. The members declared a recess while they all had their look. This action may not have been regarded as a token of respect, but it was at least recognition of the fulsome power of a woman. No one at Table 50, except the guest, ever drank liquor. They ate, drank coffee, and talked.

Whenever an argument tangled itself into a dispute, with all parties refusing to compromise their position, Runyon was called upon to assume his role as Chief Justice of the Supreme Court. His decisions were seldom questioned, but when they were, Damon threw a roll of bills on the table. Because he considered his memory more of a

sure thing than a horse or a prize fighter, Damon was always willing to underwrite his judgments with a bet.
After one of his provocative questions or remarks had
caused the desired emotional reaction, he would retire
from the conversation and observe the vocal eruption
with amused innocence.

Runyon often prompted the others to sound off against
Roosevelt and the New Deal. Winchell responded immediately. A Tennyson knight never mounted a white
charger to speed to the aid of a distressed damsel with
any more agility than Winchell got on his high horse when
Roosevelt was criticized. Winchell was immovable in his
views on the late President.

Once, after a sustained period of kidding, Winchell was
absent from Table 50 for a week. When Damon sensed
that Winchell's feelings might have been hurt, he left a
note in Walter's box at the hotel. "My dear Walter," he
wrote, "I feel that you might have misunderstood some of
the ribbing. It is always done with the deepest of my
affection. Damon."

One night Winchell expressed his own observation on
the opinions and predictions he fostered in his column.
"My friends should remember," he said, "that while I take
the bows, it is only me who has to take the boos."

Money was a favorite subject at Table 50. They made a
game of approximating each other's bank accounts. During
these discourses, Winchell recited an often-quoted slogan:
"Whether you are rich or poor it is always a good thing
to have the money." Runyon contributed his bit of hard-
bitten realism: "The world doesn't ask you *how* you won,
but *did* you win."

One night a press agent arrived in the Cub Room singing paeans about a new comedian he had just seen at the Blue Angel night club. Runyon wanted to know his name. "Irwin Corey," was the reply. "He's great," Runyon wrote on a note. Darryl Zanuck, of 20th Century-Fox, who was sitting at the table, showed interest. Paul Small entered into the discussion, identifying himself as Corey's representative, and began arranging an audience for his client with Zanuck. Then Small hurried to a telephone and called Corey. He introduced himself to Corey and asked permission to represent him in a picture deal.

"But I already have an agent, and you'll have to deal with him," Corey replied.

Later, when the members of Table 50 expressed annoyance at Small's aggressive tactic, Runyon passed his verdict around the table. "I've got to give Paul credit for quick thinking," Damon wrote. "Suppose Corey didn't have an agent. Small would have made a bundle of money if the deal had gone through."

Whenever a prominent guest came into the Cub Room he was invited to Table 50, where he soon found himself either engaged in an animated debate, or being maneuvered into making statements that the columnists could quote. Politicians and statesmen learned to use Table 50 as a sounding board to test their ideas, decisions, and programs before formally announcing them to the public. When a guest was assured that his remarks were off the record, he sometimes talked candidly about the off-stage drama that accompanies any big story.

The late Harry Hopkins came in to tell Winchell that Roosevelt appreciated the columnist's support; Mayor

William O'Dwyer talked about the city's police department; Adolph Berle gabbed about the State Department, and James Farley had a bagful of stories about his trip to Europe. Others came in: Supreme Court Justice William O. Douglas, Lord Beaverbrook, former Ambassador Joseph Kennedy, and assorted senators and cabinet members. Once when a guest left an item at the table that could be printed, a columnist suggested that Winchell flip a coin to determine which of the newspapermen could use it. Winchell protested loudly. "I was in the racket first," he said, "and now I've got to toss with my copycats."

William Randolph Hearst considered Runyon's columns so good that he sent a directive to all his editors, reading: "Run Runyon Daily No Cuts." Apparently some of the editors did not believe the order was to be interpreted literally. Two weeks later, Hearst sent out a second notice, reading: "Run Runyon Daily No Cuts No Matter What Serious Pieces You Have To Omit."

Whenever the columnists at Table 50 began boasting about their work, the exclusive stories they had printed, or the number of readers they attracted, Runyon reached into his pocket and displayed copies of the two Hearst memorandums. Damon did not need his voice to present his case.

Louis Sobol, a columnist for the *New York Journal American*, was sitting at the table one night lamenting the passing of the good old days, when there was an abundance of pleasure, free spending, gaiety, in the town, and a spirit of careless laughter prevailed. Runyon dissented. Sobol had been overly impressed by the mob boys of the past era.

"You and Winchell and Hellinger made it exciting—the way you wrote about it," Runyon insisted. "When did you see such a collection of celebrities gather as they do now in the Stork, at 21 and Morocco and other places?"

Sobol continued to reminisce on the former days of wonderful living. The old times at Rector's and Shanley's were remembered with fondness.

"There were big spenders in those days," Runyon agreed. "But I lived through that era. A cheap bunch dominated the speakeasy era, stinking characters; but I never saw so many exciting people around as you do these days."

When a bore somehow invaded the charmed circle, the members assumed their "who-dug-him-up" frown. Runyon would wander into the main club rooms to listen to the band. Winchell would insist that he needed a rumba lesson. One by one the others abandoned Table 50 until finally the uninvited guest was left alone. A watch was maintained on the table, and when word that the pest had vacated was passed along, the group reassembled and resumed the business at hand.

When 3:30 A.M. came at the Stork Club, Damon would rise from his chair and begin a slow pace around the floor of the Cub Room. It was a signal that he was ready for a ride. When he was able to catch Winchell's eye, Damon would make a motion with his hands as though turning a steering wheel. This sign would bring Winchell to his feet. "Who's coming along?" he'd ask. Both Winchell and Runyon had been writing stories of the adventures they found while coursing through Manhattan in the early morning. Some of the celebrities, intrigued by the stories of crime and miscellaneous excitement, stayed at the club until early morning, eager and ready to accept an invitation to join the riders.

The Runyon-Winchell tour ran from the Battery to the upper end of Harlem and cross town "nine ways from the jack." They never went into the Bronx or Brooklyn because neither of them knew the complicated interlacing system of streets in these two boroughs.

One night Orson Welles joined Winchell and Runyon on one of their routine dawn patrols. Winchell pulled away from the Stork Club and headed up Fifth Avenue toward Harlem. Life and death were locked in a continuing struggle in Harlem and the police in the area were kept busy protecting one and curbing the other. Here, as elsewhere, the age-old battle of the sexes was fought out, but the rules that weary civilization has laid down to regulate such disputes were often discarded. At such times the police appointed themselves arbitrators in the case. For Winchell and Runyon, Harlem provided a thrill, but for the police it was work.

But there was another interest in Harlem. Winchell's boyhood was here. He had been born and raised there and he was always willing to point out the landmarks that formed the history of his childhood. The car sped into Harlem. Winchell pointed to a building—the school he went to. Over there was the theater where he, Eddie Cantor, and George Jessel performed when they were kids. Orson Welles was interested in this. But the car was moving along. Over on that corner—the one under the street light—Winchell sold newspapers and magazines. Around the next corner—right on that spot—was where a car ran him down, and through this very street the ambulance took him to the hospital.

"I can personally guide you through all Winchellville inch by inch from having been briefed by him so thoroughly, though he claims I never listen," Damon remarked in a note he passed to Welles in the back seat.

Winchell lessened the speed of the car, made an X motion with his finger to mark a certain spot on the street for the attention of his companions. He had a fragment of a story to tell. It was right there that a jealous barber sat one day holding his sweetheart in his arms after taking a swipe at her with a razor. He was rocking her, singing to her like a father when the police arrived. When they gently lifted the girl from his embrace, her head fell off.

Winchell had been journeying through Harlem for so long that when he pulled up for a stop light, the loiterers on the corner recognized him. Winchell was affable and returned the greeting. He reported the radio calls that had come through thus far: a small fire on Lenox Avenue and a minor brawl on Seventh Avenue. Then Winchell discussed the full moon over Harlem; it was nice up there, shining just as big and fat over the slums as over Park Avenue.

The light changed, Winchell and the corner dwellers exchanged goodbyes, and the car moved off in low gear. They all listened attentively to the police calls. A good alarm always stimulated Winchell's reflexes, causing him to jam the car into high speed, and changing all red traffic lights to a bright green in his eyes.

A signal that a crime was in action at the Hotel Theresa came over the radio. The car lurched forward. Winchell and his passengers were off. He careened around corners at top speed as he raced to the scene of action. When the police drove up to the Theresa, Winchell was right behind them. They all rushed into the hotel together. But they were too late, the excitement was over. On the way back to the car Orson observed, "That Walter drives too goddam fast. We missed three cars by a fraction of an inch. The headlines about a car crash that knocked off Stork Club habitués would make a good story." Damon agreed that Walter had been reckless. He penciled a scolding note and handed it to Winchell. "You ought to watch what you're doing," it read. "Less than an inch and considerable good luck stood between us and headlines shouting: 'Runyon and Winchell Killed.'" Winchell drove on for a while without speaking. Suddenly he stopped the car at 116th Street and Lenox Avenue.

"What do you mean, 'Runyon and Winchell'?" Walter asked. "Do you think you should get top billing?"

Damon was quiet a moment, then his pencil began to move. "I haven't given the matter any particular thought."

"Then why did you say the headlines would read 'Runyon and Winchell Killed'? It should read, 'Walter Winchell, noted news commentator and columnist, accompanied by Damon Runyon . . .'"

Damon held up his hand in protest. While he was writing Winchell moved the car under a street light. "I've got a bigger following than you," Damon's note read. "I should get first mention."

"Oh, is that right?" Winchell countered. "Did you know my Hooper rating was over 25 this week?"

"What about seniority?" Damon asked. "I have been

around longer than you have. Besides, I know more newspaper editors than you do and they would give me a break. I'm sure it would be 'Runyon and Winchell' almost everywhere."

Orson leaned over into the front seat. He wanted to know where Welles fitted into the headline picture. Winchell and Runyon regarded him with scorn. "The headline would either read 'Winchell, Runyon, and Welles Killed,' or 'Runyon, Winchell, and Welles Killed,'" Winchell stated positively. Orson was informed that the debate was over whether Winchell's or Runyon's name would receive first play. Welles was a mere actor. Orson fell back into his seat and was silent.

"No," Winchell remarked, continuing the argument. "I would positively be on top. In fact, I have come to the conclusion that the headlines would read 'WINCHELL KILLED,' and underneath would be a subhead saying, 'Unidentified Man With Him'!"

The controversy of the headlines did not end that night. Winchell and Runyon carried it on in their columns, until they tired of the gag.

One morning the dawn patrol's tour had been particularly unexciting. It seemed as though the criminals had either declared a moratorium on crime or were not being detected in their wrongdoing. Winchell turned into Central Park.

The police dispatcher's clear, unemotional voice came from the radio:

"Assist a patrolman in West Fortieth."

"Too far south," Winchell commented. "We'll never get there in time to see any action."

"Lousy luck," Runyon said on paper. "So far, we've had nothing worth-while happen to us this evening."

The dispatcher came in again. "Twentieth precinct, Sixty-fifth and Columbus, calls for help."

"Also too far away," Winchell said.

The car stopped for a traffic light near 108th Street. Runyon tapped Winchell on the elbow and motioned him to pull over to the side of the road.

"What's up?" Winchell asked, obeying Runyon's direction.

Damon pointed into the park where the last fringes of night were being pushed aside by the coming dawn. A well-dressed man sat on a bench, his face in his hands. He was weeping. Runyon left the car and walked over to the sobbing man. He sat down beside him, took out his pencil and pad, and started a conversation. A few minutes later Runyon returned to the car.

"What happened?" Winchell asked. "Was it the torch?"

"No," Runyon said. "There's not much of a story to it. He found a strange stallion in the stall."

Riding in the late night and early morning with Winchell not only provided Runyon with the antidote for his loneliness, but became the fabric for some of his best columns. In these early morning hours Manhattan dwellers seemed to be at the horizon of their consciousness, their souls evolving, struggling, stumbling in their animal bodies. For those who could see and understand its design, as Runyon did, the life that moved when the city slept had poignant meaning.

"The women of the lower East Side of New York when

in pain or fright cry out 'Oh-h-h, Oh-h-h, Oh-h-h,' subdued and wailingly," Runyon wrote in his column.

"The women of midtown, the so-called Roaring Forties, taking in the Broadway night sector, cry more shrilly and sharply from the head, 'eee-eee-eee-eeee,' the tonal quality being more characteristic of women of the United States generally. I mean thus do women cry in Pueblo, Colorado, or Los Angeles.

"The women of Harlem cry 'ooo-ooo-ooo,' long drawn and throaty and eerie when it rises out of the quiet night. There is great pathos in the cry of the women of Harlem; there is high bloodcurdling alarm in the swift shriek of the midtowners; and vast distress in the low moan of the East Side.

"You note these things riding through the streets of the big city in the early hours of the morning with Winchell . . ."

Winchell said that Runyon reached the height of his power as a reporter in recording some of the fires they had witnessed together. Certainly, Damon was a fire buff, and showed an academic interest in the science of fire fighting. But the sight of bright, unbounded flames romping through a tenement like children at play stirred his deepest emotions.

For Damon, a fire created a paradox: the flames, pulsating, clawing, reaching their color and light into the night, had beauty and awesome power; it made him tingle with excitement and pleasure. But then there were the cries of anguish and grief when a human being became the prey of the consuming flame; the despair of the victims who had lost their homes and their property. A fire could contain all the tragedy of catastrophe. Damon also said that the fire made him lonesome for his Florida home on Hibiscus Island where he loved to smell the peat burning in the Dade County swamps.

"Of all the sounds that rise out of the big city night those attendant upon an alarm of fire are the most terrifying. It makes the blood run cold to see the fire department trucks go careening through the streets and to hear the bells clanging quickly as if urging 'hurry, hurry, hurry,' while the sniveling sirens whine 'oh-h-h-h, oh-h-h-h, oh-h-h-h' in anticipated anguish.

"But if there is freezing fright in the voice of the bells hastening to the point of call, there is also comfort in their new note as they quit the scene when the alarm proves more or less unfounded, a slow 'ding-dong, ding-dong, ding-dong,' gently asking gangway for the red wagons and seeming to murmur that everything is all right now.

"I like to follow the long trucks back to their station houses and watch the men at the steering wheels back them in. I reckon they can turn one of those things on a dime. The way they take them around corners is a caution to cats, but it is when they slide them back into the stations like a clerk slipping a long envelope back into a pigeon-hole that my admiration reaches its peak."

Sometimes the story of a fire, which would be told in a few paragraphs in the newspapers, or perhaps not even printed, would be fully reported in "The Brighter Side." A small fire, with little destructive effect, could produce its own touches of interest, for people have the ability to create danger and tragedy in their own minds, and quite outside reality. One morning a fire alarm in a tenement district turned out to be nothing more than a smoulder in a basement refuse pile. But it produced a vast cloud of smoke and drew the neighborhood sleepers into a crowd in the streets. A woman in a nightgown was standing on the fire escape of the top floor of the tenement where the fire was smouldering. Damon reported the drama of the next few minutes in his column.

"She was lunging forward on the platform of the fire escape as if making ready to jump. On the fire escapes below her were other women and some men in night dress, ghostly figures in the shadowy light of the approaching dawn. On the sidewalks stood little knots of spectators, some fully clad, others looking as if they had just leaped from their beds and put on the first thing that came to hand.

"Among them was a pudgy woman in a loose garment whose short gray hair was flying in the wind and who was walking around in an excited manner and watching the woman on the fire escape. She was babbling a stream of words to no one in particular. She had a foreign accent and was saying over and over again, 'come down mamma,' 'don't jump mamma,' 'come down mamma,' 'don't jump mamma.'

"A policeman climbed the ladder that was run up to the fire escape and took charge of the woman up there as she hung far out on the fire escape. She was hysterical and hysteria is a dangerous thing in such cases. He brought her down through the building to the street and there suddenly she stiffened all over and started to pull away as if trying to get back into the building, crying 'my baby, my baby!'

" 'Talk to her, some of you!' roared the policeman at a

group in the street who were apparently tenants of the building. 'Tell her the baby is not in there but is down here and all right. Talk to her, I say!'

"The woman had plumped herself down on the sidewalk in a sitting posture and sat there moaning until some of the other women showed her the baby, unharmed, and then she sobbed out of sheer relief and joy.

"The smoulder which was in the basement and had filled the street with odorous smoke was extinguished, the spectators and the police departed, and then the quiet of the morning was broken by the easy ding-dong of the bells of the home-going trucks saying 'all right now, all right now, all right now.'"

Occasionally, at about six o'clock, Runyon and Winchell stopped at Ratner's restaurant on Second Avenue in the vicinity of Sixth Street for breakfast. They ate chav and noodles, pot cheese, a snack of cold flounder and potato salad. Runyon could no longer taste his food, but his appetite had not diminished, and he continued to eat the vittles he had always liked.

Before Winchell drove Runyon to his hotel they made a last stop at the drugstore at 45th and Broadway for a nightcap of ice-cream soda.

Damon's eating caused Winchell so much concern that he consulted Runyon's physician on the matter.

"Look, Doc, I'm worried about Damon," Winchell began. "When we go out together he eats so much—you know how he likes to eat. Isn't that bad for him?"

The doctor shook his head. "Let him eat all he wants."

"But why?" Walter asked.

"But why not?" the doctor said quietly.

Once when Darryl Zanuck accepted an invitation to join the Winchell-Runyon team on an early morning ride, he was so impressed with the spontaneous melodrama that developed in the city streets that he told Damon and Walter they could name their own price if they would write a story for him based on their dawn patrol. Both men agreed to write the story, and the theater section of the newspapers reported that Winchell and Runyon would collaborate on a story for the movies. Winchell was quoted as saying that it would be a "sort of Grand Hotel of New York." But time ran out, and the movie was never made.

11

THE MAN IN THE SOFT WHITE FLANNELS

In the early spring of 1945, Damon had to undergo further treatment and a minor operation. Back at the Buckingham Hotel, he had to stay in bed under the care of a trained nurse. On April 13, Harold Conrad, one of Runyon's newspaper friends, was visiting him. Conrad turned the radio on and fingered the dial, hoping to find a program to entertain Damon. But every station carried the same program; over and over again they announced the news that President Roosevelt had died. Damon sat upright, gripping

[242]

the covers of his bed, realizing, in silent awe, the shock of the moment. Then he relaxed and fell back on his pillow. "That's the end of a great man," he murmured. Runyon had covered Roosevelt's four inaugurations as President. Now he called his editor and asked for permission to cover the Roosevelt funeral. The syndicate editor knew Damon was too ill to work and refused to give him the story. Damon insisted, and told him he would attend the funeral as a private citizen. Damon's doctors would not even consider his traveling to Washington. They insisted that such a trip would shorten his life considerably. Damon pleaded, cajoled, and threatened, and finally the doctors gave him permission to attend the funeral accompanied by his nurse.

Damon stood among the crowd as one of the thousands of spectators watching President Roosevelt's funeral cortege pass by. It was a warm spring day in Washington. It rained lightly for a while, and then the sun came out. When it was over, Damon trudged to the Hearst office and wrote his story.

"Washington, April 14.—The funeral cortege of the late President Roosevelt, a comparatively small, war-begrimed cavalcade, passed through the streets of Washington this morning from the railroad station to the White House, where simple religious services were held this afternoon before the body was taken to his old home in Hyde Park for burial tomorrow.

"The procession was the only touch of military pomp to the funeral of the dead chieftain of the mightiest armed force on the face of the earth.

"Hundreds of thousands of the people of Washington packed the sidewalks along Constitution and Pennsylvania

Avenues, and watched the passing of the mournful troop.

"At the corner of 12th Street and Constitution Avenue stood a well-dressed, confident-appearing man, a prosperous businessman, perhaps, with a boy in his mid-teens but tall for his years. He could look over the heads of most of those wedged in 10-deep ahead of him.

"'I remember his smile, father,' the boy was saying. 'I mean I remember it from the pictures of him in the newsreels. It was such a wonderful smile. It crinkled his face up all around his eyes.'

"'Yes, he smiled a lot,' the man said. 'I used to say he smiled to think of the way he had fellows like me over a barrel. I hated him.

"'I hated him most of the 12 years he lived in this town. I mean I hated him politically. Now I wonder why. He only did the best he could. No man could do more.'

"Against a sky of crystal, flocks of silvery planes roared overhead at intervals, gleaming in the sunlight. But when the noise of their motors had died away the whole city seemed strangely quiet.

"The shrill whistles of the traffic policemen, the clip-clop of feet hurrying over the pavements and the low hum of human voices were the only sounds and they carried far in the eerie silence.

"It was as if by signal everyone had said, 'Let us all be very quiet,' and the whole community fell into restrained mood as it awaited the passing of the funeral party this morning.

"Now the tump of drums, at first faint and far-off, but quickly getting stronger, broke the silence and then came the wail of a funeral march played by a band, and an auto loaded with officers passed, then a squad of motorcycle policemen on their machines. The street signals on the avenue kept changing to 'stop' and 'go' all through the procession.

"The people stood with their arms folded, those in back of the first row teetering on their tiptoes trying to get at least a fleeting glimpse of the procession.

"The Marine band, the musicians in white caps and blue uniforms, their great silver horns flashing, footed it along to the slow strains of the funeral music.

" 'They say he always had to wear a terrible steel brace like poor little Jackie Clark and like Cousin Nellie, too,' the boy said. 'They say he suffered greatly just as they do. Is that true, father? He must have been very brave.'

" 'Yes,' the man said, 'he suffered greatly. I read once he fought all the better because he fought in chains. He was a game man. That I always said. A very game man. No man could be gamer.'

"Then a battalion of field artillery, the soldiers sitting stiffly upright on their gun carriers which moved four abreast, the engines throttled down so that they made scarcely any noise.

" 'I remember so many little things about him, father,' said the boy. 'I remember his nose-glasses. I often wondered how he kept them on his nose, even when he was out in a storm. He never seemed to mind what kind of weather it was.'

" 'Yes,' the man said, 'I guess all the people will remember little things about him in the years to come. I once said that when it came to weather he didn't mind hell or high water if he had to put one of his ideas across. But it was a snide remark. I made too many snide remarks about him in his lifetime.'

"Movie cameramen on trucks weaved along the line of march. The crowd watched in silence.

"And now at last came the flag-swathed casket on an artillery caisson drawn by six strapping big gray horses in brightly polished harness, four of them mounted by soldiers.

"The President's flags were borne just behind the caisson and then came the automobiles loaded with the great men of the nation. But with the passing of the casket, the crowd began breaking up, still strangely silent. They had seen the funeral cortege of a fellow citizen, who in other nations and other times would have had the death panoply of a Caesar but who, as it was, probably had more than he would have wished.

" 'I remember when he got his little dog Fala,' the boy said. 'I think they must have loved each other a great deal, father, as much as my Mugs and I love each other. You could tell it in the newsreels when they were together. I think he must have been a very kind man to be so nice to a little dog. I hope they take good care of Fala.'

" 'Yes,' the man said, 'he was a kind man. He was kind to many people. I used to say I hated him when he was alive but now it is difficult for me to pick out any one reason why. How could I hate a kind man?' "

Many of Runyon's friends believed that the conversation between the boy and his father in the story was designed as an apology for the bitter and violent attacks that most of the country's newspapers had directed against Roosevelt, and for his own doubts about the late President.

When he had finished his story Damon immediately boarded the New York train. It was a weary, lonely trip home. His memory went back into 1921, and the October evening he had sat up all night at the wake of his old friend William "Bat" Masterson at Campbell's Funeral Parlor. It had been a strange experience, with the yellow lights of the funeral parlor making the room soft, and comfortable; the men in their blue serge suits and black ties stepping softly; their faces clean and close-shaven. He had sat near the casket remembering what he knew of the life of Bat, who had lived as a boy in Kansas, and later fought against the Comanches and Kiowas in the same Indian campaigns with Damon's father. Bat had been a Jack-of-all-trades . . . a hunter, a scout, the owner of a trading post, a sheriff, a restaurant keeper, a faro dealer, the owner of a gambling house, a deputy United States marshal and finally, a newspaper reporter.

Damon could not recall now whether or not he had fallen asleep during the wake. Perhaps he had been in a trance when the vision came. He insisted that it had been a vision, for there in the funeral parlor all his friends— the friends he knew at the time and those he came to know later—passed in review before him. There was no expression on their faces as they moved through and around each other, solemnly shaking hands. They filed by the casket, each looking at the face of the corpse, and then faded out of view. Damon was there, too, and when he passed the casket, he realized that he was regarding his own features, pale and still against the silken pillow of the coffin. It was his body that was laid out in state.

There was nothing in Damon's experience to explain

this vision; he could not reason its cause, for no part of him that he understood had ever delved into mysticism. He had played the role of the cynical reporter admirably well, he thought; yet he had never gone to the extreme of denying God, or castigating religion as a sham. He believed in God, and a personal immortality, but he supported the religions of the humble sinners who do the best they can. He knew the efficacy of prayer, and he was not ashamed to write about it in his column.

"Some people think that only by getting down on your hunkers can you pray properly," Damon wrote. "I do not agree. I think you can pray just as well walking down the street, or sitting in the movies, or eating your dinner, though I agree that the accepted posture on the knees seems more respectful. It is the attitude of humility.

"However, I do not think God is so austere that He would reject prayers not rendered from the knees. I do not think that He approves any more heartily of supplications from petitioners in loose night robes crouched on hard floors in chilled bedrooms and running the risk of pneumonia than He does the prayers from 'neath the warm covers.

"I do not believe that volume of prayer is of any special weight with God. I do not think that a vast praying of a multitude gathered together under one roof reaches the ears of God any speedier than the inward supplication of some lonely fellow in the quiet of his room.

"I do not think that where you pray or how you pray makes any particular difference, that the God who notes the sparrow's fall will listen to you wherever you are and that He will not be critical of your praying style and technique.

"I have seen the lips of men move under stress of emotion at the gaming table and I believe that they were praying. I do not question the propriety of praying under such circumstances or under any other circumstances. I think gambling is sinful when it involves the distress of the gambler's family or the impairment of his own morals, and it is conceivable that through prayer he might have a revelation that would be to his spiritual benefit.

"The man who would deny that prayer helps a person in mental or physical distress is an idiot, and if you ask me by what right I presume to set myself up as an authority on prayer, I can tell you that I have prayed for miracles and seen them happen."

Harold Conrad received a call from Runyon one day, insisting that Conrad keep the evening free for dinner. He was instructed to be in Damon's room at the Buckingham by 6 P.M. Conrad obeyed his orders and appeared at Damon's door promptly at six. He looked around the room, expecting a surprise, but finding nothing amiss, gave Runyon a quizzical look. Damon went to his typewriter, and motioned Conrad to stand behind his shoulder. Damon wrote: "Do you know what day this is?"

"Sure, it's Tuesday," Conrad replied.

Damon shook his head in annoyance. "Just as I thought," he typed. "Tonight is the night before Yom Kippur. This is the night of the feasts before the twenty-four hours of fasting. This is a very solemn holiday and as a Jew you should never forget it. Tonight we are going to a kosher restaurant downtown and tomorrow we fast."

Conrad shrugged his shoulders in surrender to Damon's decision. They went to the restaurant, where Damon ordered his favorite kosher dishes. When the meal was finished Damon scribbled another note. "There are a few facts on which I would like to enlighten you. You don't have to start fasting until sundown tomorrow, but since we're both late sleepers, we're having our big meal tonight. Now if you think this is silly, don't do it, but I feel that this holiday must have some special significance."

Conrad said he didn't think it was silly, but he would like to know when Damon had decided to espouse the faith of Judaism.

Damon ignored this remark. "I think a guy ought to get together with himself at least once a year. This is as good a time as any for you, and I'm taking a piece of it myself."

Damon had an academic knowledge of many faiths, which amazed his friends who limited their devotion to one religion. Damon was a man of all religions and used the one that best suited his purposes at the time.

In "The Brighter Side" published on February 23, 1946, Damon wrote:

"I am not afraid of dying.

"It is just the manner of dying that gives me concern.

"Naturally, I would prefer 'waking up dead' as we used to say back in my old home town of Pueblo, which means not waking up at all . . ."

But Damon found one disadvantage to dying in this manner; it ruled out the possibility of uttering any famous last words that friends might quote years after his demise—words like those credited to Wilson Mizner, who, when the hospital nurses and internes pushed an oxygen tent into his room, is supposed to have said, "Well, this looks like the main event."

"I doubt that when I exit it will be on a line as pat as

that of Bill's, though maybe some of my friends will quickly think up something picturesque and stirring for me, as is often done on these sad occasions. I know that investigation has developed that many famous last words were not actually uttered by the departing characters to whom they have been attributed, though, personally, I consider such probings uncalled-for.

"I mean, I think a man is entitled to the best curtain tag line his friends can give him, whether he utters it or not. Who has time or inclination to think up speeches when they are about to check out, anyway? And who would be there to take down his last declamation if he had one except the nurse who, the chances are, would be snoring lightly in a chair 'neath the night lamp?"

On June 17, 1946, by a decree granted in Miami, Florida, Damon was divorced by his wife. Before the spring of 1945, Damon had made only casual and affectionate references to Patrice in his column. But on April 7 of that year he wrote a caustic little piece explaining why he could never again mention his wife in future columns. With light, but pointed, touches of sarcasm, he wrote that his wife was shy and retiring by nature and he had no wish to insult her by turning her into a public character. Three days later the last sentence in his column read: "Getting married is being married, all right, all right, all right, all right."

On the night the newspapers carried the story that his wife had divorced him, Damon was sitting with his comrades at Table 50 in the Stork Club.

"What a day this has been for me," he noted on his pad.

The members of Table 50 nodded sympathetically.

Then he handed them a second note. "Yes, what a day," it read. "My horse, Scribe, came in at Jamaica. Paid $10.20."

This touch of sophisticated disregard for the end of his marriage may have impressed his friends, but Damon knew it was superficial. An hour later Damon suggested that Table 50 adjourn to an East Side night club to hear Tommy Lyman sing. Whenever a person on Broadway was carrying the torch, he found it necessary to his existence to hear Lyman sing "Melancholy Baby." Damon was still in love with Patrice. He continued to write to her, hoping to win her back. But his attempts were futile.

By an ironical coincidence, the same day that the divorce was announced, Damon, reviewing his own book, *Short Takes,* in his column, admitted another defeat. If the meaning of his column was sincere, it was a more serious defeat, at least in his own mind, than his loss of the woman he loved. For he now had doubts about the value and achievements of his life's work; he seemed to fear that he may have wasted his talents in the pursuit of material comforts.

"I do not commend the book for its literary qualities. It contains enough gummed-up syntax to patch hell a mile. But as a study in the art of carrying water on both shoulders, of sophistry, of writing with tongue-in-cheek, and of intellectual dishonesty, I think it has no superior since the beginning of time. . . .

"Damon Runyon in a simulation of humor often manages to say things which, if said in a serious tone, might be erased because he is not supposed to say things like that. By saying something with a half-boob air . . . he gets ideas out of his system on the wrongs of this world which indicate that he must have been a great rebel at heart but lacking in moral courage. . . . The newspapers of today are full of high-wire walkers like the Runyon of *Short Takes* . . . he is a hired Hessian of the typewriter . . . a distinguished . . . defeatist. . . .

"He has one not easily acquired trick which is conveying a thought by indirection. He makes it appear that he is not personally responsible for the thought, but there it is . . . I tell you Runyon has subtlety but it is the considered opinion of the reviewer that it is a great pity the guy did not remain a rebel out-and-out, even at the cost of a good position at the feed trough."

During July 1946, Winchell dedicated his vacation to the activities of the dawn patrol. Instead of ending their tour of the town at 6 A.M., Winchell drove Runyon around town until nine in the morning. This continued for a few weeks, and then Winchell complained that this new schedule was ruining his health. Runyon took Winchell to task in his column.

"I think Winchell is about to collapse, and will have to spend the remainder of his vacation in bed," Damon wrote. "It is because of bad match-making on his part.

"He picked me as his companion under the impression that he could put me to bed after two or three hours of travel every morning and retire himself saying he had to quit because Runyon was worn out, the poor old guy, thus preserving his reputation as an iron stayer-upper, which is his greatest boast.

"He did not know that I was an assistant Caliph when he was still writing little squibs for the Vaudeville News.

I used to patrol Manhattan Island in the dawnings with the late James J. Johnston, the fight manager.

"We would ride in Johnston's gray Stutz which he drove more by force of personality than skill from Child's restaurant in West 34th street, the downtown haunt of the fight mob in those days to 125th street in Harlem, stopping at every door that showed a gleam of light where Johnston would inquire:

" 'What are they saying about me?'

"At the start of Winchell's vacation we would not fold until 9 or 10 o'clock, but here lately he has been calling King's X an hour earlier, until now he is down to 6 A.M. . . . I think he will have to take a vacation from his vacation."

On November 18, 1946, former Mayor James J. Walker died. Runyon prepared to cover his funeral, but this time his doctors were obstinate. His protestations were in vain; he was unable to wangle permission to cover this assignment. The long night of his illness had now settled over him. Reluctantly he retreated to his bed in the Buckingham, where the doctors stilled some of his pain by keeping him under the influence of drugs. As Damon had predicted, Winchell had been forced to go to Florida for a rest. He called daily for information on his friend's health. One day his column read: "Runyon being ill is like New York Bay— with the Statue of Liberty dark."

In the twilight of his restless sleep and suffering, Damon made one insistent demand: that he be allowed to go for a ride. Finally the doctors seemed to relent, and gave Damon permission to take his ride. A carful of doctors and friends of Damon's accompanied him. The car moved slowly through the midtown streets of Manhattan, and then up Broadway, and then east on Sixty-second Street. When the car stopped in front of the Memorial Hospital, Damon, bewildered, and afraid, scribbled on his note-paper: "What's this?" A doctor explained that it was imperative that he now be hospitalized.

On the street Damon turned to the collection of doctors and friends. His mouth moved the sounds of a voiceless, eerie whisper. "Where's Walter? Where's Walter? He wouldn't let you do this to me." Then Damon turned, resigned and hopeless, and walked the steps into the hospital.

On his hospital bed Damon wrote a note to his son, reminding him that his name was Damon Runyon, Jr., and that he should carry that name with dignity in his chosen profession. He also wrote a letter to Patrice. He wrote his last wish on a pad. "I desire that my body be cremated and my ashes scattered over the island of Manhattan, the place that I have truly loved and that was good to me."

And there was one scribbled note to his friends. "You can keep the things of bronze and stone, and give me one man to remember me just once a year."

On December 7, he descended into unconsciousness, and three days later, at 6:10 P.M., Damon Runyon died of cancer.

On December 18, 1946, an airplane piloted by Captain John F. Gill took off from La Guardia Field. Damon Runyon's son, his daughter-in-law, and Captain Eddie Rickenbacker, president of Eastern Air Lines, and an old friend of Damon's, were the passengers. The plane headed north, banked over Woodlawn Cemetery in the Bronx, where Runyon's first wife is buried, and then soared over the

Statue of Liberty. It turned again and moved toward Times Square. The plane was at 3000 feet, moving over Manhattan, when Captain Rickenbacker opened the window of the pilot's cockpit, and tilted the urn holding the ashes of Damon Runyon. For a moment they held their unity in the wind, and then disappeared into the gray dusk of early winter hovering over the city.

EPILOGUE

Before he died Damon made a bet that he would return after his death. A Broadway pal laid Damon $1000 to $10 that Damon was wrong.

"Most persons will no doubt say that I have a bad bet. I think I have a good one. In any event, could I resist the price?"

Damon explained in one of his columns how he happened to make the bet.

"It all started at a sidewalk session at Broadway and Fiftieth when the name of a departed brother came up and someone recalled that he had promised to return after death and visit his old friends.

" 'So will I,' I remarked, sociably.

" 'You will?' said the wise guy, emphasizing the 'You' as much as to say that no matter who might return I am the least likely to enjoy that privilege.

" 'Yes, I will,' I said, stiffly.

" 'I would like to lay you ten thousand to a nickel that you don't,' said the wise guy.

" 'You have a wager,' I said to the wise guy . . ."

But the wise guy demurred on the price, Damon recalled, and said he would have to revise the odds because he was afraid he would not be able to pay off if Damon won. The wise guy did some calculating on an envelope, and then went into a drugstore near by to make a tele-

phone call, possibly, Damon speculated, to find out what
his lawyer thought of the bet.

"The best I can offer you is a thousand dollars to ten,"
the wise guy said when he returned, and Damon accepted
the bet.

"I feel that I would be a sucker not to return to a world
that has treated me well, all things considered; that has
given me much pleasure and many thrills including the
most pleasant of all, which is the winning of a good bet.
I have heard a big gambler say that next to winning a bet
his greatest thrill is losing one, but I cannot go along with
that philosophy. I hate losing. It makes me angry with
the whole world.

"It is in memory of my pleasures and my thrills only that
I will return and it will not be in grisly mood or manner or
to the accompaniment of weird rappings in darkened
rooms for morbidity is not the atmosphere I have pursued
in this world. It will be all a-grin but you are not to tell
this to the wise guy because I am saving up a big laugh
against him."

In a sense, Damon has won his bet, for he is still very
much among us. Shortly after his death, a group of his
friends, at the instigation of Walter Winchell, launched
the Damon Runyon Memorial Fund for Cancer Research.
By the summer of 1948, contributions from people who had
joined in the war against this disease had reached the two-
million-dollar mark. The work now going forward to rid
mankind of this common danger is a fitting memorial to
the man who had the common touch.